FAITH
VICTORIOUS

Faith Victorius

Phillips, Richard D.

pbc. 1

FAITH VICTORIOUS

Finding Strength and Hope from Hebrews 11

RICHARD D. PHILLIPS

P U B L I S H I N G
P.O. BOX 817 • PHILLIPSBURG • NEW JERSEY 08865-0817

Typesetting by Michelle Feaster

Printed in the United States of America

Library of Congress Cataloging-in-Publication Data

Phillips, Richard D. (Richard Davis), 1960–
     Faith victorious : finding strength and hope from Hebrews 11 /
Richard D. Phillips.
          p.   cm.
     Includes bibliographical references and indexes.
     ISBN 0-87552-515-6 (pbk.)
     1. Bible. N.T. Hebrews XI—Commentaries. 2. Faith—
Biblical teaching. I. Title.

BS2775.53 .P45 2002
227'.8707—dc21

                                              2002074943

To

MATTHEW HOLDEN PHILLIPS
Beloved son and brother in Christ
(1 John 5:4)

and to

THE CHAMPION OF OUR SALVATION
Who for joy took up the cross
(Heb. 12:2)

CONTENTS

PREFACE

There can hardly be a subject of greater importance to the Christian than that of faith. Therefore, the teaching contained in the eleventh chapter of Hebrews is among the greatest in the Bible. Here we find explained and illustrated some of our most pressing questions: What is faith? How do we get faith? What are faith's benefits? What are faith's trials and obligations? Particularly in our present time, when counterfeits to true faith abound, a study of the Bible's primer on faith is imperative for those who seek a solid place to stand.

Another great need today is an increased biblical literacy. Do we know the people and events of the Bible, especially of the Old Testament? Have we grasped the lessons their accounts contain, which the New Testament says "occurred as examples" for us (1 Cor. 10:6)? Hebrews 11, which presents many choice examples from the Old Testament, serves as an excellent crash course for those seeking entrance to the fascinating, essential world of Old Testament revelation.

The Book of Hebrews was written more than nineteen centuries ago by an unidentified apostolic leader. It was sent as a written sermon, a "word of exhortation" (Heb. 13:22). Its first audience was Christians struggling with the threat of difficulty and persecution, with the danger of falling away from the faith that alone can give salvation. The same is true, in large measure, of its readers in every generation, including today. Then, as now, these examples of faith give strength to all of us who sometimes struggle to go on believing and who like them must hold fast to Christ if we would be saved. In all their rich diversity and valuable instruction, each of these accounts from Bible history points to the same God, the same Savior in Jesus Christ, and the same calling to victorious faith as we follow him.

My goal in writing these studies is the same expressed so well by the writer of Hebrews himself: "Let us hold unswervingly to the hope we profess, for he who promised is faithful. And let us consider how we may spur one another on toward love and good deeds" (Heb. 10:23–24). May God bless these studies to all who read them, that they may trust firmly in him until the end.

These messages were first prepared as part of a series on the Book of Hebrews preached in the early morning services of Tenth Presbyterian Church in Philadelphia, in the winter and spring of 2001. As always, I thank the session and congregation of Tenth Church for their prayers, support, and encouragement for the wide ministry that allows me to prepare books like this one. I especially appreciate the love and fellowship of the many who gathered with me before the Lord's Table weekly during these early services.

This book is dedicated to my oldest son, Matthew Holden Phillips, with prayers to God that he might advance in the faith, growing to the full stature of a man of God. I am grateful to his mother, Sharon Phillips, whose patient ministry to me and alongside me in the church is such a joy to behold. Sharon also helped me prepare the discussion questions for each chapter. I am again indebted to my friends Bruce Bell and Jen Brewer for their invaluable help in reading and critiquing these chapters, and to my assistant, Patricia Russell, for innumerable helps. Finally, I give thanks to God for the wonderful gift of faith that unites me with the reader and with these Old Testament heroes in blessed communion with Jesus Christ, God's only Son, our elder Brother, and the Savior of sinners. May he find faith upon the earth, to the glory of his name.

ONE

WHAT IS FAITH?

HEBREWS 11:1–3

Now faith is being sure of what we hope for and certain of what we do not see. This is what the ancients were commended for. By faith we understand that the universe was formed at God's command, so that what is seen was not made out of what was visible. (Heb. 11:1–3)

The Christian life is the life of faith. Faith is the issue on which the matter of salvation depends; it is the key that turns the lock on the door to eternal life. Faith is the channel by which we receive the benefits of Christ's saving work; it is the cup into which God pours his saving grace.

The eleventh chapter of Hebrews is that portion of Scripture that deals most clearly with the matter of faith, most carefully defines its nature, and most exhaustively describes its working. This chapter is to faith what the thirteenth chapter of 1 Corinthians is to love, which is why it is so treasured by God's people and so frequently studied. Hebrews 11 is the work of a master teacher and loving pastor who is convinced that the fate of his readers hinges on their faith. If they are to enter into eternal life, he knows, it will be through the possession and the exercise of faith and that alone. We see his concern in the verses that immediately precede this chapter and are intimately connected to its purpose:

> *You need to persevere so that when you have done the will of God, you will receive what he has promised. For in just a very little while,*
>
>> *"He who is coming will come and will not delay.*
>> *But my righteous one will live by faith.*
> *And if he shrinks back,*
>> *I will not be pleased with him."*
>
> *But we are not of those who shrink back and are destroyed, but of those who believe and are saved. (Heb. 10:36–39)*

It is through faith, by believing, that we are saved and through want of faith that we are lost. John Owen, in his commentary on Hebrews, ably tells us why:

> *Faith alone, from the beginning of the world, in all ages, under all dispensations of divine grace, has been the only principle in the church of living to God, of obtaining the promises, of inheriting eternal life, and continues to be unto the consummation of all things. . . . Spiritual life is by faith, as are victory, perseverance, and salvation; and so they were from the beginning.*[1]

In Hebrews 11, therefore, we will devote ourselves to a thorough study of faith, which the Westminster Confession calls "the alone instrument of our justification" (11.2). Hebrews 11 is an enjoyable chapter, presenting a brilliant series of examples and connecting us to some of the greatest episodes of the Old Testament. But it is also a chapter with a purpose. Its aim is that we would emulate the faith of these heroes of Scripture so that the salvation they received would be ours as well.

WHAT IS FAITH?

Hebrews 11:1 is an oft-quoted and oft-memorized definition of faith: "Now faith is being sure of what we hope for and certain of what we do not see." This is not a comprehensive definition of faith—there are important truths about faith that are not mentioned here—but it serves as a well-crafted introduction to all that the writer of Hebrews wants us to consider in this chapter.

The first thing verse 1 teaches is the environment in which faith exists and works. It says, "Now faith is being sure of what we hope for and certain of what we do not see." The situation in which faith takes place is that in which things are hoped for but not yet possessed or manifested. In this respect, faith deals with the future. Paul spoke of this in Romans 8, writing, "Hope that is seen is no hope at all. Who hopes for what he already has? But if we hope for what we do not yet have, we wait for it patiently" (Rom. 8:24–25). Faith concerns unseen spiritual realities, things as they are in God's sight, though unseen by us. Faith, therefore, relates to the things we do not yet have, to the things we hope for and do not see, to things that are promised by God but are so far unfulfilled in our experience.

Scholars translate Hebrews 11:1 in a variety of ways. The

reason is that the key word in the opening clause, *hypostasis*, carries with it a number of shades of meaning. In the Septuagint, the Greek translation of the Old Testament commonly used by the apostles, *hypostasis* occurs twenty times to translate twelve different Hebrew words. The New International Version translates it here as "being sure," while the King James Version has it as the "substance" of things hoped for. The New American Standard and the New Revised Standard translate it as "the assurance," and J. B. Phillips calls it "full confidence."

Philip E. Hughes's excellent commentary on Hebrews lists four main ways we may take *hypostasis*, all of which have something to offer. The first corresponds to the way it is used in Hebrews 1:3. There, this same word describes God's *substance* or *being*: "The Son is the radiance of God's glory and the *exact representation* of his being." This is the idea that comes across in the King James Version of Hebrews 11:1, "Now faith is the substance of things hoped for." The point is, as Hughes says, that "faith lays hold of what is promised and therefore hoped for, as something real and solid, though as yet unseen."[2] By faith, therefore, we possess things that are hoped for; faith is the manner in which we hold them, and by faith they are made real to our experience.

That is the idea of faith emphasized in the second half of verse 1, where we read that "faith is being certain of what we do not see." The key Greek word there is *elenchos*, which the New International Version translates as "being certain" and which normally means proof or evidence or attestation of "things that are not yet seen." These things are not seen, but their proof is found in our faith. One of the reasons many scholars favor the translation of *hypostasis* as "substance" is because they see a parallel between the first and second halves of this verse. Faith is the "substance of what we hope for and the evidence of things not seen."

Clearly this idea is important to the writer's thought. He is going to make much of the example of Abraham, who lived as a pilgrim in the land of promise. Although others occupied and controlled that land during his life, he nonetheless possessed it by faith. His faith gave evidence to him of what was promised but not yet seen. The same held true with regard to the promise of a son. God changed his name from Abram (father of a nation) to Abraham (father of many nations) by virtue of the promise he possessed by faith, although he was at that time still childless. This, then, is how faith functions. It makes real to us and gives us possession of things that are hoped for but are not yet part of our experience.

The second way we may take *hypostasis* is as a *foundation*. The construction of the word lends itself to this, combining the prefix *under* with the word for "standing." It is that which stands under something else, as a foundation to a building. This is the way Augustine understood our passage, that faith is the beginning that contains the certainty of the end. By faith we begin what we will ultimately conclude by possessing and seeing.

Third, *hypostasis* may be taken as *confidence* or *assurance*, which is how the majority of translations render it. This definition deals with what faith is, namely, a confidence or an assurance in things hoped for but not yet seen. This is how the word is used in Hebrews 3:14, the other occasion where it appears in this letter: "We have come to share in Christ if we hold firmly till the end the confidence we had at first." Faith, then, is our attitude toward our circumstances, particularly toward uncertainty and want. Paul wrote, "We live by faith, not by sight" (2 Cor. 5:7). By faith we live as if things were other than they appear, because of what God has said.

Finally, this word may be rendered as *guarantee* or *attestation*. Faith, in this sense, is the title deed to things we do not possess but hope for in the Lord. One commentator writes:

> Faith is a guarantee of the heavenly realities for which we hope; not only does it render them certain for us, but it envisages them as rightfully belonging to us; it is, in itself, an objective assurance of our definite enjoyment of them. Consequently, faith "takes possession by anticipation" of these heavenly blessings and is a genuine commencement of the divine life.[3]

Faith is our guarantee that provides a foretaste of the spiritual blessings that ultimately we will know in full.

I have said that this word *hypostasis* can be taken in at least four ways, and so the question may arise as to which one is right. It seems that the writer of Hebrews deliberately chose a word that has a broad and rich array of meanings, all of which are to the point. Faith is the substance of things hoped for, it is the foundation upon which they are brought into being, it is a confident attitude toward those things God has promised, and faith is the guarantee that gives us a sure possession even now.

WHAT GOD COMMENDS

When it comes to understanding and defining faith, there are two basic approaches we may safely take, two basic questions for which we may find an answer. The first of these has to do with what faith does, and the second addresses what faith is. If the question concerns what faith does, the answer is that it makes real to us things that are otherwise unreal to our experience; it presents to our hearts things that cannot be seen with our eyes. John Calvin writes eloquently on this point, and I want to quote him at some length:

> The Spirit of God shows us hidden things, the knowledge of which cannot reach our senses. . . . We are told of the resurrection of the blessed, but meantime we are involved in corruption; we are declared to be just, and sin dwells within us; we hear that we are blessed, but meantime we are overwhelmed by untold miseries; we are promised an abundance of good things, but we are often hungry and thirsty; God proclaims that He will come to us immediately, but seems to be deaf to our cries. What would happen to us if we did not rely on our hope, and if our minds did not emerge above the world out of the midst of darkness through the shining Word of God and by His Spirit? Faith is therefore rightly called the substance of things which are still the objects of hope and the evidence of things not seen.[4]

If that is what faith *does*, the answer to what faith *is* must be closely related—faith is confidence in those things that are not present to us but are promised in the Word of God. If we believe, we are acting upon things that are not yet manifest but that we accept as true.

Noah believed there would be a flood with no other evidence than the word of God. That was faith. Think of Abraham dwelling as a pilgrim long years on end, because he held his citizenship in the city to come. Think of Moses going down in such worldly weakness to demand that Pharaoh release the tribes of Israel. These believers show us authentic models of faith, namely, a confidence that translates into action despite all the testimony of the world. Watchman Nee, the Chinese evangelist, is right to conclude:

> Faith is always meeting a mountain, a mountain of evidence that seems to contradict God's Word, a mountain of apparent contradiction in the realm of tangible fact . . . and either faith or the mountain has to go. They cannot both stand.[5]

Those who put their faith in God and in his Word, not in this world and the evidence it presents, are those whom God receives. This is the point stressed in Hebrews 11:2, which indicates where the author of Hebrews is taking us in this chapter: "This is what the ancients were commended for." What will follow in this chapter is the record of those men and women God commends in Scripture, starting in the Book of Genesis. What we are to note in each and every case is that the one thing that brought people God's commendation was their faith. Not their gifts, not their attainments as such, not their beauty or strength or popularity among men—these are the things that bring people the commendation of the world. This, by the way, is why the men and women we will study in Hebrews 11 are unnoticed and unrecorded in the secular histories. What the world admires is power, wealth, worldly glory, fame. Thus you will find no great monuments to Abraham and the others, no tablets celebrating their lives in the libraries of ancient empires, because what they had is of no account to the world. But their faith in God, though scorned by men, made them great in the eyes of the Lord and brought them his commendation and approval. Here in this chapter we see God's record, his hall of fame. The obvious point, therefore, is that if we want God's favor, God's approval,

God's commendation during these brief years of our lives, then it will come only by the possession and exercise of faith.

FAITH PERCEIVING ITS CREATOR

The method our writer takes in this chapter is to follow the record of the Old Testament as it presents different men and women of faith. To this end he begins, in Hebrews 11:3, with the opening chapter of Genesis, finding proof of his doctrine even in the creation of the world. "By faith," he says, "we understand that the universe was formed at God's command, so that what is seen was not made out of what was visible."

His point may seem obscure, but it is one that is especially germane to our times. Even the nature of the universe, the creation or beginning of all things, cannot be explained by evidence that is available to our eyes. Without faith we cannot even explain the world in which we exist.

Ours is a time committed to atheism, that is, to a view of the universe and history that excludes God. Nowhere is this lifeview more evident than in our attempts to address the origins of the universe. Undoubtedly the most popular answer today is the big bang theory, which says the universe was caused by a massive outward explosion of an incredibly dense mass. But that begs the question What caused the big bang? That is a question scientists leave unanswered. Ravi Zacharias observes:

> We have an "ontologically haunted" universe—an uncaused reality that exists which is unlike any other physical reality that we know. This has to be something more than physical. . . . A strictly physical or natural explana-

tion is not provable by the laws that govern a physical or natural universe. . . . Something beyond a physical reality is needed to explain this universe.[6]

Only faith provides an answer, for the Christian and for the atheist. The non-Christian's faith is in the big bang. As Dallas Willard observes, " 'The bang' has stepped into a traditional role of God, which gives it a nimbus and seems to rule out the normal questions we would ask about any physical event."[7] For the materialist, the big bang has taken on divine qualities that rule out questions regarding its origin. The Christian, however, finds the answer not in this kind of scientific mysticism but in the Word of God. Genesis 1 tells us that, as Hebrews 11:3 says, "the universe was formed at God's command, so that what is seen was not made out of what was visible." The universe was formed from nothing by the Word of God, who alone existed before creation.

Here the writer of Hebrews seems to be appealing to God's Word as the object of our faith. If God's Word, he suggests, was capable of creating everything out of nothing, then surely that Word is a sufficient ground for our hope. I am without peace, but God promises me peace in his Word (Phil. 4:7), the same Word that made everything out of nothing. Surely it will make peace for me, and so I believe that Word. God's Word promises victory (1 John 5:4), but I feel defeated. Isn't that Word, which created galaxies, sufficient for my faith? The same holds true for life and joy and salvation; although we do not see them, we see God's Word, we remember the power of that Word, and we rest our hearts in it.

This is how we distinguish biblical faith from the popular notion of faith as a leap in the dark. Our belief is not an exercise in blind trust, wishful thinking, a mere manifestation of our positive attitude. We believe the Word of God, because it is the Word of the God who made all things, and who, as Hebrews 1:3 tells us, "sustain[s] all things by his powerful word."

Our faith, therefore, feeds upon the Word, the way Jesus described when tempted by the devil: "Man does not live on bread alone, but on every word that comes from the mouth of God" (Matt. 4:4). Our faith grows strong from the Word and rests secure in the Word and bears fruit from the Word, which, as the writer of Hebrews has said, "is living and active" (Heb. 4:12). Ours is not a blind faith but a faith that sees by the light of God's sure revelation, a faith that says with the psalmist, "Your word is a lamp to my feet and a light for my path" (Ps. 119:105).

THE CENTRALITY OF FAITH

Let me conclude by drawing out some of the implications of what this passage says about faith and its centrality to the Christian life.

First, let us observe that if what we read here is true, faith is how we receive the blessings of salvation. What are these unseen things that our faith grasps? First is our justification, the forgiveness of our sins and the imputation of Christ's righteousness to us. There is only one way to receive and to know and then to grow into full assurance of our acceptance with God, and that is through faith in his Word. Romans 8:1 tells us, "Therefore, there is now no condemnation for those who are in Christ Jesus." And yet our conscience condemns us, the world rejects us, and the devil accuses us at every opportunity. How are we then to receive the blessing of acceptance with God, justification in Christ? The apostle John puts it this way, that even when our hearts condemn us, "God is greater than our hearts" (1 John 3:20). His acceptance, promised through his Word, overrules even the condemnation we feel for our sin. We receive this by faith alone, by faith in God's Word, which says, "Therefore, since we have been justified through faith, we have peace with God through our Lord Jesus Christ" (Rom. 5:1).

The apostle Paul begins Ephesians by praising "the God and Father of our Lord Jesus Christ, who has blessed us in the heavenly realms with every spiritual blessing in Christ" (Eph. 1:3). He goes on to outline some of those blessings, namely, our election in Christ, our adoption as heirs of God in Christ, our holiness in God's sight, our redemption through Christ's blood, and the forgiveness of our sins, all because of God's grace (Eph. 1:4–7). How do all these become real to us, how do they make a difference in our lives, how do they give us joy and hope and strength and love? The answer is by faith, which is receiving and being sure of them because of God's Word. All these things become ours through the channel of faith. What God asks us to do is believe the gospel of his Son and thereby to be saved; only through faith are we to know the benefits of what Christ has achieved for us.

We receive the blessings of salvation only through faith. Second, faith sustains us in the midst of trial and difficulty. We find an excellent example of this in the life of the apostle Paul. At the end of his life he wrote to Timothy and told what happened to him at his trial before Caesar:

> At my first defense, no one came to my support, but everyone deserted me. May it not be held against them. But the Lord stood at my side and gave me strength, so that through me the message might be fully proclaimed and all the Gentiles might hear it. And I was delivered from the lion's mouth.

The Lord will rescue me from every evil attack and will bring me safely to his heavenly kingdom. (2 Tim. 4:16–18)

The strength that sustained Paul comes only through faith in Christ and in God's Word. John Bunyan, at the beginning of his long imprisonment for preaching the gospel, begged of God that if he might be more useful to him at liberty, God would allow him to go free, but if he would be more useful in prison, then God's will be done. Clearly God thought him more useful in prison, and, armed with faith, there Bunyan wrote *Pilgrim's Progress*, which has so blessed the church for hundreds of years. Only through faith do the people of God ever find strength and courage to stand up against the world and the trials of this life. This is the kind of Christianity our world needs, the kind this world always needs, a Christianity made bold by the reality of faith.

Third, faith makes us pleasing to God and useful to others in this life. This is what we are going to find all through our studies of these biblical examples set before us in Hebrews 11. As Hebrews 11:2 tells us, it is for faith that the ancients were commended by God. That is what got these men—Noah, Abraham, Moses—into the Bible. None of them were perfect or sinless, but all of them served the Lord by faith. Writing about Moses, J. C. Ryle says:

> *In walking with God, a man will go just as far as he believes, and no further. His life will always be proportioned to his faith. His peace, his patience, his courage, his zeal, his works—all will be according to his faith.*[8]

Ryle then catalogues a number of great Christians, such as John Wesley and George Whitefield and Robert Murray

M'Cheyne, and points out that faith made them great. Some people would say, however, that prayer strengthened them, to which Ryle asks, "Why did they pray so much? Simply because they had much faith. What is prayer, but faith speaking to God?" Others will account their success to diligence and labor, to which he replies, "What is Christian diligence, but faith at work?" Perhaps it was boldness, but "what is Christian boldness, but faith honestly doing its duty?" Would we, therefore, like to be pleasing to God and useful to those around us? Ryle commends to us faith, concluding:

> Faith is the root of a real Christian's character. Let your root be right, and your fruit will soon abound. Your spiritual prosperity will always be according to your faith. He that believeth shall not only be saved, but shall never thirst, shall overcome, shall be established, shall walk firmly on the waters of this world and shall do great works.[9]

Let us, therefore, pray with the disciples, "Increase our faith!" (Luke 17:5). Let us realize that nothing is more valuable to us, nothing is more beneficial, nothing is more to be desired from God than the faith that saves us through union with Christ. It is faith that sustains in the wilderness of this world, and only faith will make us pleasing to God and useful to his kingdom. If we believe that, if we want that, then we will give our time, our effort, our favor to those things that build up our faith, scorning all those things that stand opposed.

Of one thing we may be sure, God will not deny faith to those who seek it of him. "Ask," Jesus said, "and it will be given to you; seek and you will find; knock and the door will be opened to you. For everyone who asks receives; he who seeks finds; and to him who knocks, the door will be opened" (Matt. 7:7–8).

TWO

FAITH
JUSTIFYING

HEBREWS 11:4

By faith Abel offered God a better sacrifice than Cain did.
By faith he was commended as a righteous man,
when God spoke well of his offerings. And by faith he
still speaks, even though he is dead. (Heb. 11:4)

One of the things we will discover as we study this great
eleventh chapter of Hebrews is the variety of things
faith does or accomplishes. We often think of this chapter
as focusing on the heroes of the faith, on the people themselves, and the writer of Hebrews does draw upon the wonderful histories of the Old Testament and therefore its
personalities. But ultimately it is not these men and women,
in all their variety of experience, who are on display, but
rather the one faith that shows its various facets in their col-
lective lives. Through these historical and biblical figures,
the author personifies the faith he is commending, and we

thereby see all the various things faith does and the benefits it conveys.

In our first study we saw two things that faith does. First, in verse 1, faith makes present and real things that are future and unseen. By faith we presently lay hold of our possessions in Christ. Second, in verse 3 we found that faith sees the Creator behind the creation; by faith we understand who made and sustains the universe. On through this chapter we are going to see the various things faith does. Faith pleases God, it does good works, it looks upon a heavenly city, it trusts God's promises, it conquers over obstacles. This is what the apostle John had in mind at the end of his first epistle: "This is the victory that has overcome the world, even our faith" (1 John 5:4).

CAIN AND ABEL

In verse 4, on which this chapter will focus, the writer tells us that "by faith Abel offered God a better sacrifice than Cain did." This refers to the episode recorded in Genesis 4:1–5.

> Adam lay with his wife Eve, and she became pregnant and gave birth to Cain. She said, "With the help of the LORD I have brought forth a man." Later she gave birth to his brother Abel.
>
> Now Abel kept flocks, and Cain worked the soil. In the course of time Cain brought some of the fruits of the soil as an offering to the LORD. But Abel brought fat portions from some of the firstborn of his flock. The LORD looked with favor on Abel and his offering, but on Cain and his offering he did not look with favor. So Cain was very angry, and his face was downcast.

Our text says that because of faith Abel's sacrifice was better than Cain's. There are two ways to understand this statement. The first is that because Abel was a man of faith and Cain was not, God accepted Abel's sacrifice while rejecting Cain's. The issue was not the sacrifices but the men. John Calvin holds this view, writing, "The sacrifice of Abel was more acceptable than that of his brother only because it was sanctified by faith. . . . Where did his pleasing come from other than that he had a heart purified by faith?"[1]

You see the logic of this view, a logic we want to heartily endorse. God receives the man of faith and therefore his offering, rejecting the man who lacks faith. The apostle Paul spoke this way when he wrote in Romans 14:23, "Everything that does not come from faith is sin." In Galatians 5:6 he added, "The only thing that counts is faith expressing itself through love." According to that standard we see that because he lacked faith, whatever Cain offered had to be rejected, while faithful Abel's offering was received.

We want to affirm that way of thinking, but it does not seem to be a sufficient explanation for what we find in Genesis 4. The Old Testament text seems to emphasize the difference between the two offerings, and not merely between the two men. It wasn't that the two brothers brought the same offering, one that was received because of faith while the other was rejected for unbelief. No, the offerings were different, and in that difference we see the faith of one and the unbelief of the other.

We might begin by asking whether God had given commands or regulations at that time concerning the type of sacrifice his people were to offer him. "Just what," we ask, "had God revealed to these first children or to their parents, Adam and Eve?" The answer brings us back to the prior chapter, and specifically to Genesis 3:21.

Genesis 3 tells the terrible story of man's fall into sin. Verses 1–7 record how the serpent deceived the woman so that she ate the fruit from the forbidden tree, then how Adam ate it with her and joined her in transgression of God's commandment. Verses 8–12 relate God's confrontation of our first parents in that primordial sin and their sad attempt to shift the blame even as they confessed their deed. In verses 14–19 come God's curses, first on the serpent, then on the woman, and finally on Adam. Then, in verse 21, we see God's action to deal with the problem of their sin, a response we must consider central to God's message of salvation, because it is his most direct response to sin: "The LORD God made garments of skin for Adam and his wife and clothed them." God dealt with their sin by slaying an innocent animal, a spotless substitute. God had said that sin would produce death, and here we see that it did—not the death of Adam and Eve, although death did come upon the race, but the death of a substitute who would shed its blood in their place and offer its innocence to clothe their guilty stains. The great evangelist George Whitefield rightly connects this to Jesus and his death upon the cross:

> What were the coats that God made to put on our first parents, but types of the application of the merits of the righteousness of Jesus Christ to believers' hearts? We are told that those coats were made of skins of beasts. . . . those beasts were slain in sacrifice, in commemoration of the great sacrifice, Jesus Christ, thereafter to be offered. And the skins of the beasts thus slain, being put on Adam and Eve, they were hereby taught how their nakedness was to be covered with the righteousness of the Lamb of God.[2]

In this way, God revealed the manner by which sinful humanity was to approach him. Here he taught sinners what kind of sacrifice they ought to bring. This is how we must evaluate the fitness of Abel's versus Cain's offering. "Cain brought some of the fruits of the soil as an offering to the Lord." There must have been much to commend such an offering to Cain. Here was a portion of what arose from his hard-fought labor. God had said to Adam in his curse, "By the sweat of your brow you will eat your food" (Gen. 3:19). So what Cain brought to God came only by hard work, just as farming continues to demand today. Furthermore, it must have been beautiful, pleasing to the eye just as it would have brought water to the taste buds.

What, then, was the problem with Cain's offering? The problem was that it did not involve the shedding of blood. This was the key difference between Abel's offering and Cain's. "Abel brought fat portions from some of the firstborn of his flock." Abel, in keeping with the pattern God had established with his parents and undoubtedly told to him by Adam and Eve, brought a sacrifice that pointed to the atoning death of a spotless substitute. By faith Abel's sacrifice was better than Cain's, not just because Abel's faith made it better, but because by faith he offered the sacrifice God had established as the means by which he would meet with and receive sinful humankind.

THE ONE WAY

We learn several lessons from this episode. First, we see that sinful people are justified, that is, accepted by God, only by faith in the blood of the sacrifice God has provided. This is by no means a strange doctrine to the Book of Hebrews, but one the writer has repeatedly stressed. Hebrews 9 speaks about the blood of Christ, which opens up heaven for those who trust in him. "Christ was sacrificed once to take away the sins of many people," says Hebrews 9:28. Hebrews 7:27 tells us about the meaning of the cross: "He sacrificed for their sins once for all when he offered himself."

This means that you cannot come to God any way you choose. You do not just say you believe in God and then decide for yourself how you will draw near to him. That was Cain's problem. He wanted to decide the terms of his coming to God; he offered a sacrifice according to his own devising. How bitter it was when God rejected him and his self-righteous worship.

There are only two kinds of offerings, two ways to come to God—those that point to our work, our merits, our righteousness, and those that point to Jesus Christ, crucified in our place to pay for sins. Unless we come to God confessing the guilt of our sin, our need for his grace, and embracing the gift of his Son to die in our place, we reject the one way he has provided. We then will be rejected, we then will be condemned for our sins, we then will suffer the eternal pains of hell. But people nonetheless persist in rejecting the way provided by God, especially in churches that deny or downplay the gospel. James Montgomery Boice wrote of this in his commentary on Genesis:

> That is the problem with so many "good, religious people." They come to God with their heightened sense of esthetics and want to be received by God because of their beautiful offerings. But God rejects them and their godless worship. There is no blood, no Christ and, hence, no true Christianity, however beautiful their service might be.[3]

We should offer our best to God. We should offer beautiful worship to him because he is deserving of our best. There is no higher privilege than for us to do all we can to honor and bless his name. But this comes only after the blood, only as we confess our guilt and place our faith in the blood of the sacrifice. Boice continues:

> If one comes first through faith in Christ and his shed blood, then he can present all the beautiful things he is capable of finding or creating. And God will be pleased by this, because the person does not trust these things for salvation but rather is offering them to God just because he loves him and wants to show affection. It is only on the basis of the sacrifice of Christ that one can come.[4]

You may say you are coming to God by any of a number of means. You may say you are coming because of your sincere heart. You may say your religion is based upon your good works. You may trust sacraments or religious tradition or church membership. But apart from the blood of Jesus Christ all of these will be rejected, like Cain's offering, because you have not come by faith in the way God has provided. The apostle Peter said to the Sanhedrin, "Salvation is found in no one else, for there is no other name under heaven given to men by which we must be saved" (Acts 4:12). Jesus had taught, "I am the way and the truth and the life. No one comes to the Father except through me" (John 14:6). These passages refer not merely to some vague belief regarding Jesus Christ but to his blood, to which Abel's sacrifice pointed and on which it relied, his substitutionary death in our place upon the cross. As Hebrews 9:22 tells us, "Without the shedding of blood there is no forgiveness."

JUSTIFICATION BY FAITH

If there is any doubt about the importance the writer of Hebrews attaches to faith, Hebrews 11:4 removes any ambiguity. Here he tells us that it was by faith that Abel was declared to be righteous. The New International Version blurs this somewhat, saying, "By faith he was commended as a righteous man." The New American Standard is better here, saying that by faith "he obtained the testimony that he was righteous." A literal reading of the Greek would be that "by faith he was declared to be righteous."

By faith Abel was declared righteous, or was justified, by God. This is one of the great teachings of the Bible, the doctrine of justification by faith. This is why these early Hebrew Christians, the original recipients of this letter, were exhorted to not abandon their faith, as they were tempted to do, because by faith in Christ alone are sinners justified by God. This doctrine is at the core of the gospel, the good news regarding what God offers us in Christ, because it declares exactly what we see in the case of Abel, how a sinner can be accepted and declared righteous by the holy God.

This is what John 3:16 declares, that "God so loved the world that he gave his one and only Son, that whoever believes in him shall not perish but have eternal life." By believing on Jesus Christ, by resting on his saving work for the forgiveness of our sins, by accepting God's Word and coming to him the one way he has provided, we are forgiven and are, as our text says, "declared righteous by faith." Not by works, which declare our supposed merit—that was Cain's mistake and the cause of his rejection—but by faith, which declares our need and our acceptance of God's gracious gift.

We find this truth emphasized in the Genesis account.

Abel was a sinner, being the son of Adam and bearing sin's corruption in his fallen human nature. Yet when he came to God bearing the blood of a substitute, "the LORD looked with favor." The blood turned away God's wrath by speaking of the forthcoming cross of Christ, and on that basis God received Abel with gladness. This was something available not only to him; Cain could have been justified this same way. In Genesis 4:6, God explained to a bitter Cain, "Why are you angry? Why is your face downcast? If you do what is right, will you not be accepted?"

Justification by faith makes the same claim to everyone reading these words. It is not just some of us who were born into Christian families, who have the right connections, who have the proper appearance or works or money to offer, but all of us who may come in this way. That is what God said to Cain: "Why do you not come in the way I have graciously provided?" God offers each and every one of us salvation, forgiveness of sin, and restoration unto fellowship with him, by the way of the sacrifice he has provided, even the blood of his Son.

If you study the early chapters of Genesis you will find that this point is forcefully made. We have seen the first sacrifice, when God clothed Adam and Eve with the skins of the innocent animals, in Genesis 3:21. Although Adam did not die, his sin barred him from the Garden of Eden. Verses 22 and 23 tell us he was no longer fit to dwell with and serve God there, to eat from the tree of life and live forever. But then verse 24 adds a remarkable detail: "After he drove the man out, [God] placed on the east side of the Garden of Eden cherubim and a flaming sword flashing back and forth to guard the way to the tree of life." East of Eden, into the curse-blasted world of sin went Adam and Eve, their way back barred by angels with flaming sword.

That imagery would become important later in Israel's history, in the time of Moses, when instructions were given for the construction of the tabernacle, the place where man came to meet with God. The tabernacle was where God dwelt in the midst of his people. At its center, in the Holy of Holies, rested the ark of the covenant, God's throne on the earth, where he kept the tablets of the Ten Commandments, his law.

The tabernacle was a movable structure, made of wooden frames and curtains. The writer of Hebrews makes a careful study of it in Hebrews 10. There was an outer court where sacrifices were offered and the priests were cleansed before entering. The outer room, called the Holy Place, was where the priests served. Finally, there was the inner sanctum, the Holy of Holies, where God dwelt, separated by a thick veil from sinful humankind. What is striking, when we read the instructions in the Book of Exodus for its construction, is that the image of cherubim was to be worked into the curtains of the tabernacle: "Make the tabernacle with ten curtains of finely twisted linen and blue, purple and scarlet yarn, with cherubim worked into them by a skilled craftsman" (Exod. 26:1). This detail evidently carried great significance, because it is repeated four times in the book (Exod. 26:1, 31; 36:8, 35). Just as the cherubim guarded the way to God in the garden with a fiery sword, so did the curtains in the tabernacle keep sinners away.

It seems from this that after their sin and expulsion from the garden, Adam and Eve still came to worship God, and it was to the guarded way between the cherubim that they came with sacrifices of blood. Likely this is where Abel and Cain came, one with a sacrifice of blood and the other with an offering representing his works. Abel would have been like the priests of Israel in days to come, able to come to the gate, to the Holy Place, to live and serve in God's reflected light, but barred from the inner sanctum by the guardian angels, just as the thick veil with their image of cherubim kept Israel's priests out from the Holy of Holies.

But that is not the end of the story. The Book of Exodus gave more instructions for the tabernacle, about the mercy seat, the atonement cover for the ark of the covenant within the Holy of Holies.

> Make an atonement cover of pure gold—two and a half cubits long and a cubit and a half wide. And make two cherubim out of hammered gold at the ends of the cover. Make one cherub on one end and the second cherub on the other; make the cherubim of one piece with the cover, at the two ends. The cherubim are to have their wings spread upward, overshadowing the cover with them. The cherubim are to face each other, looking toward the cover. Place the cover on top of the ark and put in the ark of the Testimony, which I will give you. (Exod. 25:17–21)

Although no sinner could come directly into God's presence, just as neither Adam nor Abel could return into the garden, there was one day of the year, the Day of Atonement, when Israel's high priest could enter into the Holy of Holies. This one day prophesied an age to come. And when the high priest came, he was confronted by the sight of the two cherubim. The atonement cover of the ark of the covenant graphically portrayed the gate to the garden. There two of the mighty angels faced each other, with wings upswept, casting down the shadow of their presence. Their eyes gazed downward, to the ark, which contained the tablets of the law of

God, broken by sinners as by Adam and Eve before. They saw that man is barred from the garden, from the tree of life, from the presence of God. Because he is a transgressor, man is under the sentence of death and therefore must not enter back into life.

But on that Day of Atonement, the high priest came and poured the blood of the atoning sacrifice upon the mercy seat between the cherubim. And thus the way that was barred now was opened. This provides us an insight about the guardian cherubim: they not only kept shut the way to God without the atoning blood but also secured that way for the great day to come when the true sacrifice would open wide the gates to paradise. That one day a year when the high priest came before the cherubim with a blood offering symbolized an age that would be opened by the true High Priest with the true blood he had shed. God therefore said to Moses, concluding the commands God gave for the mercy seat: "There, above the cover between the two cherubim that are over the ark of the Testimony, I will meet with you" (Exod. 25:22).

God met with his people between the cherubim, not in the garden but at its gate. God met with them at the place where the blood was poured to cover the breaking of the law. Between the angels on the ark of the covenant sat the mercy seat. In Greek this is the *hilasterion*, the term the apostle Paul used in Romans 3:25 to describe what God presented to us in the death of Jesus Christ. "God presented him as a *hilasterion*," that is, a mercy seat, or as the New International Version puts it, as "a sacrifice of atonement." This tells us that what the angels were looking for all along was Christ, whose coming would end their watch, and therefore they guarded the way to God until his coming.

That great day for which the angels looked did come. The Gospels tell us about it. The day came when the curtain with its cherubim was not merely pulled aside temporarily but torn from top to bottom, removed altogether, the angels thus relieved of their ancient task. Matthew tells us of the death of Christ: "And when Jesus had cried out again in a loud voice, he gave up his spirit. At that moment the curtain of the temple was torn in two from top to bottom" (Matt. 27:50–51).

Finally, the true High Priest had come to the gate between the cherubim, and there he offered once for all his blood. The gate was opened; the angels rejoicing went their way, taking with them the sword of death. Now the way is open wide and secured by Christ, and he is the way. Now it is to him that we come. It is through him that we come not merely to the gate but into the garden to walk with God. Between the cherubim, Abel was declared righteous by faith because he looked to the sacrifice to come. Now through faith in Christ every sinner can come to be accepted into fellowship with God and to receive everlasting life.

WHAT ANGELS LONGED TO SEE

Our verse in Hebrews concludes by saying of Abel, "And by faith he still speaks, even though he is dead." Faith bore testimony to Abel, that he was accounted righteous, and Abel bears testimony even today about faith—about its value, about its worth, about its power to justify those who trust in Christ.

Shortly after his faithful offering Abel was killed. Cain tried to silence his testimony; we learn in Genesis 4:8 that instead of repenting Cain murdered his brother to put away the testimony about faith and the righteousness it brings. And yet the man of faith speaks still in the Word of God to us. Faith in God is never silenced, because God keeps the testimony of his own alive.

When I think of Abel I often recall Peter's statement in the first chapter of his first epistle. Speaking of the gospel he said, "Even angels long to look into these things" (1 Peter 1:12). Abel's faith spoke to those angels. It declared to them a wonder, that sinners might come back to God, that those under the curse might meet with him at the place they guarded. What a wonder it was to the guardian cherubim when Abel by his sacrifice of faith was accepted and approved of God.

The same must have happened when Abel was killed, the first man to die but also the first to appear in heaven. What an event that must have been! For the first time a sinner appeared in the holy courts of glory, but cleansed and clothed in the righteousness of God's Son. How the angels there must have marveled at this mystery of grace! G. Campbell Morgan writes:

> It was a great occasion when this first soul representing a fallen race, appeared in the unsullied light of the home of the unfallen. He came by faith, ransomed by love, at the cost of sacrifice. As the Scripture declares that "the angels desire to look into" these things, this must indeed have been a mystery of life and love demanding their close attention, and not perchance, even fathomed by them, until the explanation . . . was wrought out upon the Cross of Calvary.[5]

Before the time of Jesus Christ, Abel spoke, though dead, of a sacrifice yet to come that would take away our sin, of faith in the sacrifice that declares the sinner righteous. Now that Christ has come, he speaks of it still, with a voice that fully rejoices. Many of our hymns approximate the words that Abel, though dead, must speak about his Savior. Horatius Bonar's words would be welcome and familiar to the lips of Abel, who brought a sacrifice of faith in the work of the Savior's blood:

> Not what my hands have done
>   can save my guilty soul;
> not what my toiling flesh has borne
>   can make my spirit whole. . . .
>
> Thy work alone, O Christ,
>   can ease this weight of sin;
> thy blood alone, O Lamb of God,
>   can give me peace within. . . .
>
> No other work save thine,
>   no other blood will do;
> no strength save that which is divine
>   can bear me safely through. . . .
>
> I praise the God of grace;
>   I trust his truth and might;
> he calls me his, I call him mine,
>   my God, my joy, my light.

Thus speaks the voice of Abel. And so shall we, if we are justified by faith in that same blood, clothed in that same righteousness, and thus accepted into the love of God just as Abel was before us.

THREE

FAITH PLEASING GOD

HEBREWS 11:5-6

*By faith Enoch was taken from this life, so that he did not expe-
rience death; he could not be found, because God had taken him
away. For before he was taken, he was commended as one who
pleased God. And without faith it is impossible to please God,
because anyone who comes to him must believe that he exists and
that he rewards those who earnestly seek him. (Heb. 11:5–6)*

The Westminster Shorter Catechism is famous for its first
question, "What is the chief end of man?" and its answer, "The chief end of man is to glorify God and enjoy him
forever." Of all the people depicted in Scripture, apart from
our Lord Jesus Christ, there is no one whose description
more closely attains this standard than that of Enoch, the
seventh in the line from Adam. So dear was this man to the
heart of God that God took Enoch to himself without demanding that he suffer the pains of death. It is no surprise,

therefore, to find Enoch in this procession of heroes of the faith.

The account of Enoch's life in Genesis 5 makes no mention of his faith. Yet his faith seems to motivate the statement in Hebrews 11:6, that without faith it is impossible to please God. The idea is that we can be sure Enoch was a man of faith, because otherwise he could never have pleased God the way he did.

Hebrews 11 presents its heroes of the faith in chronological order as they are found in the Bible, yet several commentators point out that there is probably more at work than a historical progression. It appears that there is also a topical progression to the points their stories make about the life of faith. That is especially true of the three men who lived before the great flood—Abel, Enoch, and Noah.

Andrew Murray, for example, describes them as Abel, the *sacrifice* of faith, Enoch, the *walk* of faith, and Noah, the *work* of faith.[1] That is a progression supported by the Bible. First, you are brought into a right relationship with God by trusting the sacrifice he has provided in the blood of Christ; second, having been brought into relationship with God, you then walk with him by faith; third, and only then, do we talk about the works of faith, the practical good deeds that follow as a result.

Another writer, A. W. Pink, sees these three figures combining to provide "an outline of the life of faith." He writes, "Abel is mentioned first not because he was born before Enoch and Noah, but because what is recorded of him in Genesis 4 illustrated and demonstrated where the life of faith begins. In like manner, Enoch is referred to next . . . because what was found in him . . . must precede that which was typified by the builder of the ark."[2] Pink's outline depicts faith's *worship* in Abel, faith's *walk* in Enoch, and faith's *witness* in Noah.

It is hard to say that the writer of Hebrews had this kind of explicit outline in mind since he does not put it that way himself. It seems that he is mainly following the biblical order, with each portrait making a particular point about faith. However, it does seem that the divine Author has placed them together in such a way as to build the progression of which Murray and Pink speak. Pink reminds us of the importance of a biblical ordering of the Christian life, writing:

> *Witnessing and working ("service") is what are so much emphasized today. Yet dear reader, Heb. 11 does not begin with the example of Noah. No indeed. Noah was preceded by Enoch, and for this reason: There can be no Divinely-acceptable witness or work unless and until there is a walking with God! . . . And this, in turn, must be preceded by Abel's worship of faith.[3]*

ENOCH, WHO WALKED WITH GOD

In the last chapter we saw that Abel was declared righteous by faith, since he came to God through the blood of Christ. Now we turn to the walk of faith with the life of Enoch. The Bible says very little about this man. All that we have comes from the genealogy in Genesis 5:

> *When Enoch had lived 65 years, he became the father of Methuselah. And after he became the father of Methuselah, Enoch walked with God 300 years and had other sons and daughters. Altogether, Enoch lived 365 years. Enoch walked with God; then he was no more, because God took him away. (Gen. 5:21–24)*

What we know about Enoch, therefore, is that he was the seventh patriarch before the flood from the line of Adam through Seth. When he was 65 he had a son named Methuselah. He then lived a total of 365 years, after which he mysteriously departed from the earth without dying. Think of all the information we do not know about this man—this doesn't seem to be much of a biography. But the Bible tells us one vital fact that speaks volumes. Twice in these verses we are told, "Enoch walked with God." That wouldn't make a bad inscription on a gravestone. It tells us much about the character and the pattern of this man's life. Far more important than the job titles he held or his attainments in life was that he walked with God.

What does it mean to walk with God? First, this speaks of a living relationship, a companionship between a man or a woman and God. It implies personal knowledge, an ever-increasing understanding of the one with whom you walk. It implies agreement of mind and heart. The prophet Amos rightly asked, "Do two walk together unless they have agreed to do so?" (Amos 3:3). There is an intimacy, a fellowship, and surely a joy of company between two who walk together. When it is God with whom we walk there is a hierarchy, just as when the disciples walked with our Lord Jesus Christ. One is the Lord; the other is disciple. One is teacher; the other is student. One is Father; the other is child.

There can hardly be a more beautiful description of the Christian life than the idea of walking with God. The great Puritan, Thomas Watson, said of it:

> To walk with God is to walk by faith. We are said to draw nigh to God (Heb. 10:22) and . . . to have fellowship with him. "Our fellowship is with the Father" (1 Jn. 1:3). Thus

we may take a turn with him every day by faith . . . "They shall walk in the light of thy countenance" (Ps. 138:5). "Yea, they shall sing in the ways of the Lord." It is like walking among beds of spices, which send forth a fragrant perfume.[4]

Peter Lewis tells the story of a Chinese pastor who was imprisoned in a labor camp for his faith. His captors put him in charge of emptying the contents of the camp latrine. Every day he would take the foul excrement out and distribute it in a field as fertilizer. The smell was so bad that the guards drew away and gave him plenty of space as he did his work. For that reason, the pastor came to love his lowly occupation, because in the resulting solitude he could talk and sing to God aloud, both of which were otherwise forbidden. He joyfully named the dung heap in which he worked his garden, singing:

> *I come to the garden alone,*
> *while the dew is still on the roses . . .*
>
> *For he walks with me and he talks with me,*
> *and he tells me that I am his own,*
> *And the joy we share as we tarry there,*
> *none other has ever known.*[5]

That is what the Christian life is intended to be, the walk of faith, the abiding fellowship with our loving God. In that way he transforms even the worst circumstances into beds of roses, simply because he is there with us. What glory this is, that when God calls us to faith in him, he invites us to walk along his side! So every day—ordinary days, difficult days, joyful days—are days with God, a foretaste of what heaven is about: to be with him, to know his love, to see his light and feel the warmth of his pleasure.

Walking with God is its own destination, and yet we are going somewhere. We are growing in our knowledge of the infinite and divine, we are growing more like him in character as he guides us, we are realizing progress in spiritual things. This is the Christian life! It's not a bare knowledge of facts, not a grim recitation of doctrines. To be a Christian is to walk with God, to know him, and to live in the light of his presence.

Our verses in Hebrews 11 do not focus on the idea of walking with God but rather of pleasing God. The explanation is that the writer of Hebrews is quoting from the Greek translation of the Old Testament, the Septuagint, and not from the Hebrew original. This Greek version, which so many apostolic writers used, is noted for its reluctance in using anthropomorphisms, that is, descriptions of God in human terms. The Bible will speak of God's arm or God's hand or the eyes of the Lord, all of which are anthropomorphisms. God has no body, he has no hands, but his functions and activities are described in human terms for our benefit.

Because of its hostility to this way of speaking, the Septuagint often removed anthropomorphisms in its translation from Hebrew into Greek. The passage from Genesis 5 on Enoch's life provides a classic example. Instead of saying that he walked with God, the Septuagint says, "Enoch pleased God." Following that translation of Genesis 5, the writer of Hebrews comments that Enoch was pleasing to God and therefore must have had faith.

We need not be troubled by this human interference in the divine Word, for the New Testament, which is divinely inspired, sanctions this reasonable interpretation of Enoch's life. We may rightly, then, take this idea of pleasing God as a working definition of what it means to walk with him. If you and I want to enjoy God's fellowship, to feel his pleasure, it is going to be out of obedience to his Word. Jesus talked about this to his disciples shortly before his departure from them. "Abide in me," he said, "and I will abide in you. . . . If you obey my commands, you will abide in my love, just as I have obeyed my Father's commands and remain in his love" (John 15:4, 10, my translation). While walking with God involves more than simple obedience to his commands, obedience is necessary and integral to any life lived in fellowship with God.

TWO ELEMENTS OF FAITH

The main point of our passage is yet another proof of the necessity of faith. Enoch pleased God and therefore was taken by God before he died, which surely would have been impossible without faith. The writer goes on, in Hebrews 11:6, to point out two vital components of genuine faith: "Anyone who comes to him must believe that he exists and that he rewards those who earnestly seek him."

The first of these statements points out that faith must have an object. Today we hear a lot about the power of faith without anything being said about the object or content of that faith. Mainly we are told to believe in ourselves, and it is true, I suppose, that self-confidence will help you accomplish many things. Surely a baseball player is more likely to hit a fastball if he thinks he can. A salesman is more likely to close the deal if he believes in his ability to do so.

But the faith the writer of Hebrews is describing differs greatly from that. At first glance it may seem that he is only asking people to believe that God exists, to hold at least some abstract assent to the idea of God. On closer study, however, he is being quite a bit more specific. A literal translation of the Greek original would read this way: "It is necessary for anyone who comes to God to believe that he is."

This wording points to the confessional or doctrinal aspect of faith in a way the original Hebrew audience surely would have noticed. The wording here is reminiscent of the basic creed of Israel, from Deuteronomy 6:4, called the Shema: "Hear, O Israel: The LORD our God, the LORD is one." That was the great confessional statement of the Jewish faith, as it still is, and the original Hebrew readers would have understood this as a way of saying, "Anyone who comes to God needs to have straight just who God is."

At a minimum, the original Jewish audience could not help but see a connection to the great statement God made to Moses at the burning bush in Exodus 3:14. Moses, having just been told to go down to Egypt and confront mighty Pharaoh, asked God, "What is your name?" God answered him, saying, "I AM WHO I AM. This is what you are to say to the Israelites: 'I AM has sent me to you.'" Again, in the Greek translation used by the early church, the link is even more explicit. In the Septuagint, Exodus 3:14 says, "Tell them I am the one who exists." Pointedly using that very language, our writer says, "Anyone who comes to him must believe that he exists."

Therefore this first element of faith has to do with its content and doctrine. Faith must identify the God of the Bible, the Lord who spoke to Moses from the burning bush, as the one true God. Faith must be in him if it is to be saving faith. Over and over the Bible says, "I am God, and there is no other" (Isa. 46:9). Faith must first agree with God's affirmation and turn to him as the only true God.

Not surprisingly, this element of faith also corresponds to the first of the Ten Commandments: "I am the LORD your God. . . . You shall have no other gods before me" (Exod. 20:2–3). This is a warning against all forms of idolatry, and especially philosophies and theologies that compete with the Bible. Whoever draws near to God, our passage says, must believe that the God of the Bible is the one and the true God, putting no others in his place.

First, then, we have the content or object of faith. Second comes the motivation of faith: "Anyone who comes to him must believe that he exists and that he rewards those who earnestly seek him." We must believe not only that this is the true God but also that we have to deal with him, that he is the Judge and Arbiter of our destiny and fortune.

As soon as you speak of God giving out rewards people get upset; they perceive a threat to the clear biblical teaching of salvation by grace alone. "If salvation is a matter of getting your reward, then we must be talking about works salvation," they reason. That, however, is very far from the case. This particular statement asserts the reality that this God is the One who determines blessing versus condemnation. To have faith you must realize and accept that you have to deal with this God, that his judgment about you is the vital one, that you had better seek him and gain his favor.

By calling this second element the motivation of faith, I mean that faith must turn to God as the One who saves, it must come to him seeking reward, seeking favor, seeking his grace. The opposite is to ignore him, to think that it doesn't matter what God thinks of you, what he intends for your future. That is what unbelief is all about. Few people deny the existence of God, but many deny the relevance of God, the need to seek him for salvation. This is demonstrably true in our day. The vast majority of people agree that God must exist, and yet they are not seeking him. Instead, they are serving other worldly gods as the source of the rewards they so highly covet.

That begs vital questions. Do you have to deal with God? Do you need to pay attention to him, to listen as he speaks, to open your heart to a relationship with him, to let him change the way you live, to make him the great hope for the whole of your life? The answer, according to God's revelation in the Bible, is yes.

Although there are many reasons why we must come to God in faith, I will give just two. First, God tells us that he is a holy Judge who will surely punish every sinner. God says that at the end of days he will cause everyone to stand before him for judgment. Revelation 20:12 paints the picture for us: "And I saw the dead, great and small, standing before the throne, and books were opened. . . . The dead were judged according to what they had done as recorded in the books."

People deceive themselves that they will fare well on that day, since they are by their assessment "basically good people." But the Bible renders a far different verdict, according to God's standard of perfect holiness. Romans 3:23 puts it directly: "All have sinned and fall short of the glory of God." Romans 6:23 tells us the consequences: "The wages of sin is death." Every person who stands guilty of sin—and that is every one of us—is in dire peril of this condemnation. For this reason you had better seek God, to find out how you might gain his favor.

That is one reason why you must deal with, as Francis Schaeffer put it, "the God who is there." A related and positive reason, and one we are confronted with in the record of Enoch, is that there is a life after this one and a God to be known and enjoyed with awe. There is a life after death, where God awaits us.

Perhaps the most interesting point about Enoch is one we have not yet considered. Enoch never died. The writer of Hebrews puts it this way: "He did not experience death; he could not be found, because God had taken him away." One day this godly man was there, and the next he could not be found. People looked for him, but he wasn't there. They may never have known what happened to Enoch, but we do. God took him from this life and into the next without having to die. There are only two people of whom this kind of thing is recorded, Enoch and the prophet Elijah, the latter of whom God swept up in a chariot of fire. The amount of speculation devoted to these matters has literally filled books, but these are the bare facts Scripture tells us, and further speculation is useless.

The point is that Enoch's record tells us of a life after death, of God's ability to reward his own with everlasting life. Indeed, that is the way we should think about the idea of rewards from God, namely, what he said to Abraham: "I am your shield, your very great reward" (Gen. 15:1). What greater reward could we ever desire more than God? F. F. Bruce rightly observes, "The reward desired by those who seek him is the joy of finding him; he himself proves to be their 'exceeding joy' (Ps. 43:4)."[6]

Our reward is the one Enoch received, namely, everlasting life with God, his free gift to all who turn to him in faith. Earlier I quoted Paul's statement in Romans 6:23, which begins with the first reason we should seek after God: "The wages of sin is death." But that sentence is completed with the second reason: "The gift of God is eternal life in Christ Jesus our Lord." That gift is what we see in the experience of

Enoch, the man who pleased God by faith, and that is the greatest motive for seeking the Lord. Just as in Abel we saw the power of Christ's death to restore us to God, so in Enoch we see the power of his resurrection life, the new life we too enter by faith in God.

SEEKING AND FINDING GOD

God rewards those who seek him. What, then, does it mean to seek God? It does not mean that we search him out the way a scientist seeks out knowledge. We are not left to follow a dim line of clues, eagerly seeking to piece together a workable theory. No, God is all around us; the evidence of his being is before our eyes this second. The whole universe is a display, as Paul says, "of his eternal power and divine nature." God is, Paul concludes, "clearly seen, being understood from what has been made, so that men are without excuse" (Rom. 1:20).

Seeking God therefore means seeking his favor, seeking a relationship with him. For sinners it means seeking forgiveness. It means coming to him confessing that we are sinners, the way David did: "Have mercy on me, O God, according to your unfailing love. . . . For I know my transgressions, and my sin is always before me. . . . Cleanse me with hyssop, and I will be clean; wash me, and I will be whiter than snow" (Ps. 51:1, 4, 7). Hyssop was a plant the priests used as a brush to sprinkle the sacrificial blood. It is another way of saying that David was coming to God, seeking forgiveness through the blood of the Christ, the Lamb of God who takes away the sin of all who come through faith in him.

But seeking God means more than seeking his favor and forgiveness, which he freely gives in Jesus Christ. It also involves a relationship with him. It means making him the God of your life, your King, your Teacher, and your Lord. It means, as Enoch shows us, to walk with God and to offer your life for his pleasure. It means seeking that which is the chief end for our lives, the purpose for which we were made, namely, the glory of God and the enjoyment of him.

Seeking God is just another expression for living by faith, which is what this great chapter is all about. Andrew Murray says this:

> Faith seeks for God; it believes that He is; it keeps the heart open towards Him; it bows in humility and hope for Him to make Himself known. To know God, to see God in everything and everywhere, in our daily life to be conscious of His presence so that we always walk with Him—this is the true nobility of man; this is the life that faith lives; this is the blessedness Jesus has now fully revealed in the rending of the veil. Faith can walk with God.[7]

What, then, will you find if you do seek after him? Enoch gives the answer. You will find life. Eternal life. That means a life that goes beyond the grave, a life in heaven. But it also means heaven in this life, in this world. It means the answer to the problem of death. God spared Enoch death because by faith he was pleasing to God. For us it means a similar triumph over death; it means that death will lose its sting. Death shall be nothing but an open door to the fullness of the life we begin here by faith. Death will mean the perfection of what here is only imperfectly attained, to walk with God, to rest in him, to delight in him, and to know his pleasure, which is faith's greatest reward.

That leaves but one last question: If you seek, can you be

sure to find him? The answer is obvious, isn't it? Our passage says God "rewards those who earnestly seek him," not that you have to find him on your own. If you seek God, he will respond to your seeking. "No one can come to me," Jesus said, "unless the Father who sent me draws him, and I will raise him up at the last day" (John 6:44). That means that if you seek God, it is because he has been seeking you, and therefore you will find him. God is drawing you into the arms of his love for the purpose of the eternal life that comes through faith in Christ. Those who seek him he rewards with himself, and those who walk with him in this life he brings to himself in the next, conquering the grave, for a fellowship of joy that will last forever.

FOUR

FAITH WORKING

HEBREWS 11:7

*By faith Noah, when warned about things not yet seen,
in holy fear built an ark to save his family. By his
faith he condemned the world and became heir of the
righteousness that comes by faith. (Heb. 11:7)*

Our studies in Hebrews 11 bring us to the story of Noah,
one of the great figures of human history. Noah shares
a distinction with Adam that every single human being is one
of his descendants, since God restarted the human race
through his family after the great flood.

The flood in which Noah was saved is one of the great
events in the history of our planet. It was an event brought on
by the greatness of humankind's sin. Genesis 6:5 says, "The
LORD saw how great man's wickedness on the earth had become," and so God expended his wrath in the destruction of
the rebel human race, saving only faithful Noah and his family. Not surprisingly, practically every religion and mythology,
from Asia to North America, remembers Noah and the flood.

A Sumerian tablet from 1600 B.C. tells how a king was warned about a destructive deluge and therefore built a great boat. In Akkadian there is the Atrahasis Epic, which tells of a great flood that destroyed humankind after earlier attempts to curb its wickedness. Only Atrahasis and his family, who were warned by the creator-god Enki, escaped in the boat they were told to build. This saga seems to have provided the source material for the Babylonian epic, Gilgamesh, which tells the same story.[1] While these and other examples are greatly corrupted by pagan ideas, they preserve a shared memory of this cataclysmic event.

Noah's name seems also to have passed down into one language after another. In ancient Sanskrit his name became *Manu*, based on the word *ma* ("water"). Thus the name is "Nu of the waters." This was passed on to ancient India, where Manu was the father of all peoples. Egyptian mythology named its water god Nu, and the mythical founder of the Germanic peoples was Mannus, from which we get the word *man*.[2]

The events of Noah's life have great theological significance. The words *righteousness* and *grace* first appear in the Bible in his account. He gives us a great symbol of judgment in the flood. His ark provides a great symbol of salvation (1 Peter 3:20). The rainbow remains an enduring symbol of the covenant—a reminder God put in the sky for himself, standing between us and God's judgment, just as Jesus now is "the guarantee of a better covenant" (Heb. 7:22).

Noah is best known today as a conservationist icon, a kind of Santa Claus for the environmental movement. The main thing associated with him is the animals he saved, but in Hebrews 11 it is faith for which he is remembered. Everything I have said about Noah proves that he was a great and significant man; yet it was his faith that made him great in God's eyes. Indeed, Noah sums up everything we have learned about faith so far in Hebrews 11. Like Enoch, he "walked with God" (Gen. 6:8–9); like Abel he was, as our passage says, an heir of the righteousness that is by faith.

A MODEL FAITH

Hebrews 11:7 begins, "By faith Noah, when warned about things not yet seen, in holy fear built an ark to save his family." This tells us that Noah is an outstanding example of verse 1's description of faith as being "certain of what we do not see." There were two things Noah believed that were unseen, the great flood God had promised and the salvation that would come by means of the ark.

The key verses describing this are in Genesis 6:

> So God said to Noah, "I am going to put an end to all people, for the earth is filled with violence because of them. I am surely going to destroy both them and the earth. So make yourself an ark of cypress wood. . . . I am going to bring floodwaters on the earth to destroy all life under the heavens, every creature that has the breath of life in it. Everything on earth will perish. But I will establish my covenant with you, and you will enter the ark—you and your sons and your wife and your sons' wives with you." (Gen. 6:13–14, 17–18)

Genesis 6:3 tells us that God spoke these words to Noah 120 years before the flood. There had never been an event like God described, nor such a boat. The ark Noah was told to build was stupendous in size—about the size of a modern battleship—and we can guess that Noah was to build it on dry ground, far from any ocean or sea. That is faith in things unseen! Even though he had not one shred of proof apart from God's word, Noah nonetheless believed. This shows that faith in things unseen is the same as faith in God's Word, the same as faith in God's promises. We believe things apart from tangible evidence, because God has so informed us and given his promise. We believe God, and that is faith in things unseen.

This kind of faith required Noah to stand alone in his generation. Apart from his immediate family members—and the strength of their faith is not clear—Noah alone trusted in the Lord. If we are going to live by faith and not by sight, that will often be true of us as well.

Noah also provides an excellent example of what we are told in verse 6, that "without faith it is impossible to please God." We know that Noah pleased God because Genesis 6:9 says, "Noah was a righteous man, blameless among the people of his time, and he walked with God." Like Enoch, Noah was an eminent man of faith, with much to say to us.

Because Noah is described as blameless, many people argue that he was justified or that he pleased God by his works. This fails to recognize what the preceding verse says, that "Noah found favor in the eyes of the LORD" (Gen. 6:8). It isn't that he was blameless and thereby found grace with God, but his blamelessness was the result of God's favor. Indeed, God's grace was the source of his faith, which in turn was the motivating power behind his works. Our verse in Hebrews 11 insists that everything Noah did was "by faith." Faith was the operating principle for all that Noah did or achieved. "By faith Noah . . . built an ark to save his family." He shows us that the same faith that brings us into a right relationship with

God through Jesus Christ also moves us to actions that please God in practical works of obedience.

Indeed, what God demanded of Noah was far greater than what he asks of us. God required Noah to believe something that had never happened before, something unprecedented and seemingly unlikely. God asks you, however, to believe things that have already happened, namely, the death and resurrection of Jesus Christ, things that were done not in a corner but in the full light of history and recorded in the Bible. Similarly, God promised to do something for Noah that was difficult to imagine, that is, his salvation through the flood by entering the ark. But God promises you something he has done countless times before, probably in the lives of people you know. He promises to forgive your sins through faith in Christ, to give you his Spirit and lead you into a new life. Some promises remain for the future, such as the resurrection from the dead. But even this lacks novelty, since it already happened to Jesus, who has gone before us in all things. Like Noah, we are saved by believing things that are not seen, and we please God only by believing his Word and trusting his promise.

FAITH WORKING

The first thing Noah shows us is a model faith that saved him and his family. Second, his example shows us that faith always results in works. "By faith Noah, when warned about things not yet seen, in holy fear built an ark to save his family."

People are often confused about the relationship between faith and works. The apostle Paul insists that we are declared righteous in Christ "apart from works" (Rom. 4:6). But the apostle James says that "faith without works is dead" (James 2:17). James goes on to say, "Show me your faith without deeds, and I will show you my faith by what I do" (James 2:18). This apparent contradiction has led many people to choose one versus the other. Martin Luther, for instance, a famous champion of Paul and of salvation by faith alone, derided James's letter, questioning its canonicity and labeling it "an epistle of straw."

However, upon closer examination, we find that there is no contradiction between Paul and James. Paul states that we are justified by faith alone. James merely qualifies that by insisting that such faith inevitably does good works, or else it cannot be true faith. "You believe that there is one God. Good!" he exclaims. "Even the demons believe that—and shudder" (James 2:19).

One of the most helpful expressions in sorting this out is a famous one from John Calvin, who said, "We are saved by faith alone, but the faith that saves is never alone." He means that true and saving faith is always accompanied by obedience, "which flows from faith like water from a fountain."[3]

Our verse specifically tells us two things that proved Noah's faith, flowing forth naturally from that fountain. The first is one word in the Greek, but three in our text: "in holy fear." The Greek word is *eulabetheis*. F. F. Bruce translates it as "out of reverent regard."[4] B. F. Westcott renders it, "moved with pious care."[5] Philip E. Hughes puts it as "taking heed" with careful attentiveness.[6] The point is that Noah had reverence for God, which led to his attentive care to the details of what God commanded.

In Genesis 6:14–21, we read a summary of quite detailed instructions about the building of the ark. Undoubtedly Noah needed such details to do the job given him. But his faith is commended by his attentive care to all that God told him. Genesis 6:22 praises him: "Noah did everything just as God commanded him."

The Puritans in seventeenth-century England were like Noah. The name *Puritan* was given to them by scoffers because of their care for studying and obeying God's Word in great detail. Then as today people think such reverent attentiveness to be narrow religion. They wrongly equate it with the attitude of the Pharisees, who made life difficult not with their biblical obedience but with their manmade restrictions. But biblical obedience does not fetter you, does not make you narrow. Rather, it liberates you to what is good and true and wholesome. That is why James speaks of "the perfect law that gives freedom" (James 1:25). Studying and following through on God's Word will not shrink you but make you grow. But the path of obedience to Christ is a narrow one, one that speaks both yes and no, one that keeps us in the ark and out of the flood. Jesus taught, "Wide is the gate and broad is the road that leads to destruction, and many enter through it. But small is the gate and narrow the road that leads to life, and only a few find it" (Matt. 7:13–14).

That was Noah's manner of life, arising from his faith. But there is one great work that flowed from his faith and served as its main evidence—Noah's ark. Hebrews 11:1 says that faith is the "evidence of things not seen," and Noah's ark was the evidence that pointed to the flood long before anyone saw the raindrops falling.

Noah's ark provides a classic demonstration of the relationship of faith to works. Why did Noah build the ark? What caused this work? It was his faith. It was "by faith" that he built the ark. That is clearly the case, because unless he believed, it would have been lunacy to do something like this.

Noah built the ark only because he truly believed that what God said about the flood was true, that the flood was going to come, and that unless he built the ark he would be drowned with everyone else.

But what if Noah had not built the ark? What would we say about his faith? Imagine Noah insisting that he believed what God had said if he were not busy working on the ark! What would we say to a faith like that? We would say what James did—that such faith is useless and dead unless accompanied by works. If Noah did not even start working on the ark, start chopping on trees and making diagrams, then the simple fact is that he could not have believed. But he did believe, and therefore he built the ark. That is how faith and works fit together.

The same is true for us. We always act according to our beliefs. Do you realize that? You always act according to your real convictions. If you believed there were a bomb in your room, you would run out of it right now. If we believe it is necessary to repent and believe the Good News to be saved, we will flee temptation and at least begin chopping at the trees of our sinful habits, while feeding our faith. It took Noah 120 years to build the ark, and it will take a while for our sanctification. But if we believe, we will at least get to work now. There is no escaping the truth: faith and works are inseparable. As Alexander Maclaren put it, "If faith has any reality in us at all, it works. If it has no effect it has no existence."7

FAITH CONDEMNING THE WORLD

Hebrews 11:7 provides a stark comparison of faith and unbelief, as viewed through Noah and his unbelieving generation: "By his faith he condemned the world." Noah can be said to have condemned the world in several ways, but before he condemned it we can be sure the world condemned him. Ray Stedman says:

> We may rightly visualize the mockery and jeering which Noah must have daily faced as he built a huge ship. He was a hundred miles from the nearest ocean, with a ship many times too big for his own needs, and when he had finished, he filled it with animals! Had he lived in our day he would have been dubbed, "Nutty Noah!" Yet Jesus used "the days of Noah" as representative of the condition of the world before his own return, and indicated that his followers must be prepared to face the same kind of scornful hostility that Noah met day after day.[8]

The Christian life seems just as nutty to an age as self-absorbed as ours. That anyone would deny himself, willingly sacrifice, and devote himself to holiness is mind-boggling to the world around us.

Noah's faith condemned the world, first of all through his witness. Second Peter 2:5 calls Noah a "preacher of righteousness." Surely he would have explained his actions, why he was building the ark, to those who inquired and went on to laugh at him. He would have warned the world of a judgment to come and offered the way of safety in the ark. Likewise, we are to teach and explain the life we lead, the truth that we believe, the judgment and salvation that are there before us as well. And in its rejection of our message, the world is condemned for unbelief.

Noah's witness condemned the world, but we can also say his faith condemned the world. There it was before their eyes, evidence of God's word, which they rejected or ignored. Ignoring Noah comes to the fore in Jesus' description: "For in the days before the flood, people were eating and drinking, marrying and giving in marriage, up to the day Noah entered the ark; and they knew nothing about what would happen until the flood came and took them all away. That is how it will be at the coming of the Son of Man" (Matt. 24:38–39). Just like today, the great mass of people paid no attention to spiritual matters, they were indifferent to God's word as it was proclaimed, and Noah's faith condemned them for their unbelief.

Calvin points out that Noah also condemned the world by his salvation:

> The fact that Noah obeyed the command of God condemns by his example the obstinacy of the world, and the fact that he was miraculously saved from the midst of death is proof that the whole world, which God would doubtless have preserved had it not been unworthy of salvation, justly perished.[9]

Noah's salvation proved that people could have been saved if they were willing to believe and put their trust in the word of God. Noah's salvation vindicated his faith and his testimony, once wickedly made sport of by the voices of the world. Alexander Maclaren pointedly remarks:

> No doubt there were plenty of witty and wise things said about him. . . . And then, one morning, the rain began, and continued, and for forty days it did not stop, and they began to think that perhaps, after all, there was some method in his madness. Noah got into his ark, and still it

rained. . . . I wonder what [they] thought about it all then, with the water up to their knees. How their gibes and jests would die in their throats when it reached their lips![10]

FAITH INHERITING RIGHTEOUSNESS

That leaves one statement our passage makes about Noah, that "by faith he became heir of the righteousness that comes by faith." There are two key elements of this statement, the first being inheritance and the second the righteousness that comes by faith.

Let me treat the second of these first. The apostle Paul speaks in similar language in Philippians 3, where he contrasts the righteousness of faith with the righteousness of the law. First he tells about his former righteousness as a Pharisee:

> If anyone else thinks he has reasons to put confidence in the flesh, I have more: circumcised on the eighth day, of the people of Israel, of the tribe of Benjamin, a Hebrew of Hebrews; in regard to the law, a Pharisee; as for zeal, persecuting the church; as for legalistic righteousness, faultless. (Phil 3:4–6)

He then places these onto a balance sheet, noting that the things he once considered assets, so far as righteousness was concerned, he now understands as liabilities. Only one asset provides the righteousness God accepts, the righteousness that is by faith. He continues:

> But whatever was to my profit I now consider loss for the sake of Christ. What is more, I consider everything a

loss compared to the surpassing greatness of knowing Christ Jesus my Lord, for whose sake I have lost all things. I consider them rubbish, that I may gain Christ and be found in him, not having a righteousness of my own that comes from the law, but that which is through faith in Christ—the righteousness that comes from God and is by faith. (Phil. 3:7–9)

The key statement is the last, in verse 9, that Paul wants not the righteousness of his works under the law—which must be flawed at best and therefore useless—but the righteousness of Christ, which comes only through faith in him. Surely the writer of Hebrews is making this point about Noah: Although he did much, he sought not a limited and imperfect righteousness of his own but the perfect righteousness from God that comes through faith.

This righteousness, we are told, came to Noah by means of inheritance. By faith he became an heir of righteousness. By faith he became a child of God. This is why it was so appropriate for him to act in a godly and righteous way, because by faith Noah was God's child and therefore destined to inherit his riches. Inheritance means that the source of the gift is without, not from his resources but from the one who grants the inheritance. That is how the righteousness of Christ comes to us, from God as an inheritance to his children and not from ourselves as an achievement. Furthermore, an inheritance is established by a fixed law and procedure. Paul speaks of this in Romans 4:16, where he says of this inheritance, "The promise comes by faith, so that it may be by grace." It is a gift, and a gift is received with open hands to the praise and the glory of the Giver.

This is what makes the righteousness of faith so secure.

When we receive righteousness as an inheritance, by the open hands of faith, it is afterward possessed as a right. It is not something that has to be protected. Children do not hold their inheritance by conquest or by cunning but as an unbreakable right inherent in their status as children of the father. In just that manner, our righteousness in Christ, received as an inheritance by faith, cannot be lost or taken away. It is as closely joined to us as a father's name is joined to his child who bears it. Ultimately our inheritance is based upon the sovereign will of God and not upon our will. That is what the apostle John wrote in his Gospel:

> To all who received him, to those who believed in his name, he gave the right to become children of God—children born not of natural descent, nor of human decision or a husband's will, but born of God. (John 1:12–13)

All that being true, how much more secure is this righteousness that comes by faith than any we might try to win for ourselves, a crown more steady than any we could have placed upon our heads, perfect and completely acceptable in the sight of the Lord.

A MINISTRY OF SALVATION

Noah's faith meant salvation to some—namely, himself and his family—and condemnation to others, indeed to all the rest of the world, which fell under God's holy wrath. But let me conclude by pointing out that the direct result of his faith was salvation, while condemnation was only an indirect consequence.

Our passage says that Noah's faith condemned the world.

Christians are sometimes encouraged by statements like this to make it their job to condemn the world; they make it their ministry to point out how rotten it is, to fascinate on the reigning sins and unite in hysteria over the latest debaucheries. But that does not seem to be the way Noah lived, and he charts a different course for us.

Everything Noah did was calculated to save. He acted as an instrument of salvation, even though his faith indirectly condemned the world. He was an ambassador of the grace of God, and that is what every Christian is to be.

Noah was "a preacher of righteousness" (2 Peter 2:5). Surely that involved a condemnation of sin and a warning of judgment, but all of that was done in the shadow of the ark of salvation. That is where Noah's real effort went. His faith set him to work upon the ark. If the world would not seek its open door, then it would be destroyed. But Noah directed his labor to salvation. Our labor must have this same influence, to commend and offer salvation to others, praying that God will grant them faith to believe and be saved. That is the labor of the Christian, by faith in the Word of God. Paul said this in 2 Corinthians 5:19–20:

> God was reconciling the world to himself in Christ, not counting men's sins against them. And he has committed to us the message of reconciliation. We are therefore Christ's ambassadors, as though God were making his appeal through us. We implore you on Christ's behalf: Be reconciled to God.

Believe, God says to the world through our faith, that a judgment is yet to come. And believe that in the cross of Christ, an ark as wide and long and high and deep as Noah's ever was, everyone who believes will find safety through the storm. Peter Lewis says it well:

> *Christ Jesus is our ark now: big enough for the whole world, strong enough to withstand the shocks of life, the rising waters of death, and the upheavals of the last judgment. There is safety here in the Son of God, sent to be for us all the shelter, the salvation, that we so desperately needed; our ark and safe passage into the new world God has planned. From that ark we will emerge to inherit a new heaven and a new earth (Rev. 21:1).*[11]

God asks that you believe, that you trust him, and through that faith he will do the rest in and through you, saving you and others from the wrath to come and carrying you to the wonderful salvation he has provided in Jesus Christ.

FIVE

FAITH LOOKING FORWARD

HEBREWS 11:8-10

*By faith Abraham, when called to go to a place he
would later receive as his inheritance, obeyed and went, even
though he did not know where he was going. By faith he made
his home in the promised land like a stranger in a foreign
country; he lived in tents, as did Isaac and Jacob, who
were heirs with him of the same promise. For he was
looking forward to the city with foundations, whose
architect and builder is God. (Heb. 11:8–10)*

Of all the studies of the life of faith in Hebrews 11, the
longest and most involved is that of Abraham, the patriarch of Israel. His is also one of the longer accounts in the
Old Testament, running from chapters 12 to 25 in the Book
of Genesis.

Abraham's significance can hardly be overestimated. It
was through him that God gave the covenant of grace, by

which we are saved. It is therefore accurate to say our salvation rests in part on God's faithfulness to Abraham. In Romans 4:11, Paul gives Abraham the important designation "the father of all who believe." Thus we are saved as the spiritual offspring promised by God to Abraham, and his faith provides a model we are bound to follow. Therefore Jesus responded to the Jews' boast that they were children of Abraham by saying, "If you were Abraham's children, then you would do the things Abraham did" (John 8:39).

In the New Testament, Abraham provides the example of faith par excellence. In the Old Testament, he is the first person to be specifically commended for his faith. Genesis 15:6 says, "Abram believed the LORD, and he credited it to him as righteousness." The apostle Paul particularly emphasizes Abraham as a model for faith. Paul's discussion of justification by faith in Romans 3 is followed in Romans 4 by a proof of his doctrine from the life of Abraham. The Book of Galatians also relies strongly on the precedent of Abraham's faith.

Given all this, we are not surprised that the writer of Hebrews pays so much attention to Abraham in this great eleventh chapter. Earlier he appealed to Abraham's example, writing of his patient faith that received God's promise (Heb. 6:13–15). In Hebrews 11 the account of Abraham runs from verse 8 to verse 19, with four different statements that begin, "by faith Abraham." We will consider his faith in four studies, beginning here with verses 8–10, a passage that begins, "By faith Abraham, when called . . . obeyed and went."

FAITH OBEYING GOD'S CALL

The story of Abraham begins in the twelfth chapter of Genesis, after a brief biography of his father, Terah, at the end of Genesis 11. We learn of God's call to Abraham in Genesis 12:1:

> The LORD had said to Abram, "Leave your country, your people and your father's household and go to the land I will show you."

Abraham's life of faith begins here for, as our passage says, by faith he "obeyed and went, even though he did not know where he was going." This was not only the beginning of Abraham's salvation but also an important beginning in the history of God's redemptive work.

We see in Abraham that faith acts in response to God's call. It is God's initiative that is emphasized at the beginning of Abraham's life of faith, God's sovereign grace that goes forth with his saving call.

It is important for us to realize that Abraham was saved not because there was something special about him but by virtue of God's sovereign choice. Abraham was not singled out because of his faith but because of God's grace. We might think he was picked because he was a good man. But the Bible argues otherwise. The prophet Isaiah writes, " 'Listen to me, you who pursue righteousness and who seek the LORD: Look to the rock from which you were cut and to the quarry from which you were hewn; look to Abraham, your father, and to Sarah, who gave you birth' " (Isa. 51:1–2). His point is that nothing in their ancestry commended them to God apart from God's gracious initiative.

Joshua 24:2–3 is even clearer: "Long ago your forefathers, including Terah the father of Abraham and Nahor, lived beyond the River and worshiped other gods. But I took your father Abraham from the land beyond the River and led him throughout Canaan and gave him many descendants." Abraham was not seeking God; he was a pagan idol worshiper when God called him. What Paul wrote in Romans 3:12 was true of Abraham as well: "There is no one who understands, no one who seeks God. All have turned away, they have together become worthless; there is no one who does good, not even one."

Therefore Abraham was saved because God sought him. His faith was preceded by God's call and responded to God's call, a call that came by grace alone by God's sovereign choice. James Montgomery Boice applies this example to us all, writing,

> In the way God called Abraham, God calls all who become his children. God comes to us when we are hopelessly lost in sin and without knowledge of him (Eph. 2:1–7). This is a universal fact in the spiritual biography of Christians. And our response is nothing more than belief in God and in his promises.[1]

That is how Abraham's story begins: "By faith . . . when called . . . he obeyed and went." He was seventy-five years old, living in Ur, the land of his fathers, at that time a thriving locality. In Acts 7:2–3, Stephen tells us, "The God of glory appeared to our father Abraham while he was still in Mesopotamia, before he lived in Haran. 'Leave your country and your people,' God said, 'and go to the land I will show you.'"

The life of faith begins when God reveals himself to us. In Abraham's case it was apparently a divine visitation. For us it may be hearing God's Word preached, or opening and reading a Bible. It may begin by seeing something compelling in the life of another person. But in every case faith begins with God revealing himself to someone lost in sin, ignorant of and unconcerned about him.

We see here, too, what faith requires. Abraham had to leave his home, his family, his prospects for life, to go where God called him. So it is for everyone who would be saved. God calls us not merely to believe some abstract facts but to obey his call and to follow him. Abraham's example shows us what real conversion looks like, namely, that there is a definitive change of life. A. W. Pink writes:

> The evidence of regeneration is found in a genuine conversion: it is that complete break from the old life, both inner and outer, which furnishes proof of the new birth. . . . The moment a man truly realizes that he has to do with God, there must be a radical change: "Therefore if any man be in Christ, he is a new creature; old things are passed away, behold, all things are become new" (2 Cor. 5:17).[2]

For Abraham this meant rising when called and going where he was commanded as a manifestation of his trust in God. Astonishingly, verse 8 tells us that he didn't even know where he was going. Abraham did not have a crystal-clear plan, a vision that mapped out where he would be in five or ten or fifty years. Rather, he met God, he heard God's call, and at great cost to himself and surely with much perplexity, he obeyed and went. Faith always demands decisive action, always manifests itself in obedience to God's command. Speaking of Abraham, James wrote about faith and works: "You see that his faith and his actions were working together, and his faith was made complete by what he did" (James 2:22). As Pink says, "Faith and obedience can never be severed; as the sun and the light, fire and heat. . . . Obedience is faith's daughter."3

We really do begin the life of faith not knowing where we are going. Most of us, Abraham included, could not handle at the beginning an awareness of all that will happen in and to us, all that will be required, all we will give up and all we will receive along the journey of faith. Like us, Abraham didn't know what was in store, but he had met God, had heard his call. He believed, and by faith he obeyed and went. That itself is more than flesh alone can ever do, and it shows that faith is a divine gift inspired and empowered by God.

Imagine what Abraham's friends and neighbors would have thought about him. As he was packing they would surely have asked, "Where are you going?" To this he could only reply, "I do not know. I have been called by God to follow him." Imagine their response, and then realize that it will be no different for you. People will ask you, if you answer God's call in faith, "Why are you giving up the pleasures of sin? Why are you throwing your life away to serve where God calls you? Why are you obeying the Bible instead doing what is popular?" You, like every believer since Abraham's time, must reply—no doubt with much difficulty—"I have met God, and he has called me, I know not where. I must obey, for I want to be saved by faith in him."

FAITH BELIEVING GOD'S PROMISE

The call to faith is always followed by the life of faith; the same principle by which we first are saved causes us to live as saved people. Thus we find, in verse 9, the description of Abraham's life in the land of Canaan:

By faith he made his home in the promised land like a stranger in a foreign country; he lived in tents, as did Isaac and Jacob, who were heirs with him of the same promise.

We have seen how difficult it is to obey God's call. But many a Christian has learned how much harder it is to live the life of faith over a period of many, many years. Abraham began by obeying God's call, and he persevered by believing God's promise. God had promised him a land as his inheritance, and Abraham's faith consisted of receiving that promise as he continued to obey and serve.

With fits and starts Abraham finally arrived in the land of Canaan, which God had promised that he would possess. However, when Abraham got there, he found that it was inhabited by the Canaanites, an idolatrous people who did not know the Lord. By faith he lived there, not as its owner but as "a stranger in a foreign country" (Heb. 11:9). He lived as a sojourner, a resident alien, in the land God had promised would be his.

This presents a classic picture of the life of faith. We have great promises from God that belong to us now but by and large have not yet been manifested in our experience. Abraham went to the land promised to him, but when he got there it did not yet belong to him. This shows us the already-not yet character of the life of faith. We possess the promises already, but they are not yet consummated in our life. This is what Hebrews 11 emphasized from the beginning, that faith is the evidence, the possession, of things not yet seen.

By faith Abraham lived in the land that was not yet his. This is what Stephen says in Acts 7:5, "[God] gave him no inheritance here, not even a foot of ground. But God promised him that he and his descendants after him would possess the land, even though at that time Abraham had no child." Like us, Abraham received the promise by faith; he literally lived upon the promise since he had not yet received the reality. Even when he had children and began to see the future take its shape, verse 9 says, "He lived in tents, as did Isaac and Jacob, who were heirs with him of the same promise." Even many years later, upon the death of his wife Sarah, Abraham had to purchase a plot of land in which to bury her—sure evidence that he was but a pilgrim in this land that God had promised would be his own.

Abraham's experience informs us that the life of faith is not one of receiving all the promises in tangible form but rather of believing them in the face of hardship, receiving them by faith, living as Abraham did out of confidence in and reliance on God. From beginning to end, the Christian life is one of faith and not of sight. Philip E. Hughes writes:

> He who begins by faith must continue by faith, for faith is the principle not only of initiation but also of perseverance. The life of faith did not cease for Abraham when he left Ur of the Chaldees behind him or when at length he set foot on the territory toward which he had directed his steps. Indeed, the situation into which he moved on his arrival in the land of promise was a more severe trial of his faith than was the call to leave home and kindred, and it was easier for him to live by faith as he journeyed toward a goal as yet unseen than to do so upon reaching this goal and finding that the fullness of all that had been promised was "not yet."[4]

I think Abraham's situation is well expressed by the salutation that begins the apostle Peter's first epistle. He was writing to early Christians who were "scattered" across Asia Minor. He thus began his letter with these words: "To God's elect, strangers in the world" (1 Peter 1:1). This description told them two things about themselves, the two things shown to us in the life of Abraham. The first is that they were living in a world not their own, as pilgrims rather than possessors, as strangers living in an alien country.

This means that Christians do not belong to this world but to another. The apostle Paul writes in Philippians 3:20, "Our citizenship is in heaven. And we eagerly await a Savior from there, the Lord Jesus Christ." Our allegiance belongs to another realm. That is what we pray in the Lord's Prayer: "Thy kingdom come, thy will be done on earth as it is in heaven." As strangers, our long-term interests are not attached to this present world, which we know is passing away. We do not find our comfort here, not because we are a difficult sort of people but because our permanent home is elsewhere and we have a growing homesickness for the place where we belong.

Being a pilgrim means that we do not love the things of this world. Colossians 3:1–3 tells us, "Since, then, you have been raised with Christ, set your hearts on things above, where Christ is seated at the right hand of God. Set your minds on things above, not on earthly things. For you died, and your life is now hidden with Christ in God." It is always good, therefore, for Christians to assess how tightly worldly things grip upon our hearts. We must take seriously what John writes in his first epistle: "Do not love the world or anything in the world. If anyone loves the world, the love of the Father is not in him. For everything in the world—the cravings of sinful man, the lust of his eyes and the boasting of what he has and does—comes not from the Father but from the world. The world and its desires pass away, but the man who does the will of God lives forever" (1 John 2:15–17).

The Puritan Jeremiah Burroughs helpfully admonishes us:

> *The Scripture tells us plainly that we must behave ourselves here as pilgrims and strangers (1 Pet. 2:11). Consider what your condition is, you are pilgrims and strangers; so do not think to satisfy yourselves here. . . . So let us not be troubled when we see that other men have great wealth, but we have not. Why? We are going away to another country; you are, as it were, only lodging here for a night. If you were to live a hundred years, in comparison to eternity it is not as much as a night, it is as though you were traveling, and had come to an inn.[5]*

Therefore we are to live as those who expect to wake up soon in the realm of glory. That is where we belong in Christ. That is the other part of Peter's salutation, which so well describes Abraham's position and ours. He writes to his readers not merely as strangers in the world but "to God's elect . . . chosen according to the foreknowledge of God the Father, through the sanctifying work of the Spirit, for obedience to Jesus Christ and sprinkling by his blood" (1 Peter 1:1–2). This is who we are, this tells us where we belong. We are God's chosen people, his elect and beloved children in Christ.

This means that though the world accounts you nothing, you are chosen of God. It is a hard truth that you do not fit in here, that the world is not likely to think much of you as you live by faith within its precincts. There is a reason why secular history records nothing of Abraham—because Abraham and what he represented were of no interest, of no appeal to the world. He was not a mighty king or a famous entertainer or a villainous rogue. These are the things that catch the eye of the world. And as you lead a quiet, godly life, you will not interest the world much either. You do not belong to it, but you do belong to God. He cherishes you, even if the world despises you—as it did our Lord Jesus Christ. God has set you apart for himself, he has sanctified you by the Holy Spirit, he has purchased you by the precious blood of Jesus to be his own.

The reality of our pilgrimage is often quite difficult for us to bear. We grow impatient for our possessions, resentful that we cannot be like the others around us. The desire to put down real roots here in this world, a weariness with the pilgrimage of faith, leads many into spiritual difficulties. That is why we must live by faith as Abraham did. We live and feed our faith upon promises, delighting in God's boundless love for us, remembering our end, which will be so different from that of this world. And while we wait, God gives us himself as our present comfort, our near companion, our saving help. As with the men of faith before him, Abraham did not make his pilgrimage alone in this world, for he walked with God. What God said to him in comfort, he also says to us: "I am your shield, your very great reward" (Gen. 15:1).

FAITH SEEING A CITY

Our passage concludes with one of the greatest statements of the life of faith, a statement that has inspired the hearts of countless believers. Verse 10 tells us what kept Abraham going all those long years: "For he was looking forward to the city with foundations, whose architect and builder is God."

It is easy for us to think of those who lived long ago as

primitives, as people necessarily possessing a feeble comprehension. But it is clear that Abraham possessed a highly developed sense of his spiritual position. What was it, we ask, that allowed this man to live so heroically in such difficulties? The answer is here: "He was looking forward. He was looking forward to the city with foundations."

Imagine how many times Abraham looked out from the flaps of his tent at some city or settlement in that land. He must have yearned for those comforts. Keen was his desire for the things offered in that land, dusty as it was, his longing to settle down, to live in peace and at rest. But our text tells us that by faith he lifted his eyes upward to better if distant things, to a city far surpassing anything set before his fleshly eyes, a city with foundations, designed and built not by Canaanite lords but by the Lord of heaven.

There is an obvious comparison between the tents in which he lived, dwellings without foundations, and the cities of Canaan with their earthly foundations, and finally the city to come, the city of God, with its eternal foundations. Abraham longed for foundations, but he chose the eternal instead of that which passes away. We can say the same about the splendor of those cities. They must have been impressive compared with Abraham's tents. But he compared them with that city of which God is the architect and builder, a city of speechless glory and infinite majesty. Abraham looked to what is to come, not contenting himself with the offerings of the world, not sacrificing his inheritance for the droppings of a dying humanity. Abraham's heart was in that city to come, and he placed his hopes there by faith in God.

Abraham applied to his situation what we often call an eternal perspective. He considered his present in light of his future inheritance with God. This is how Christian faith is sustained in the midst of deprivation and trial. John MacArthur writes:

> *The Christian . . . is willing to forsake the present glory, comfort, and satisfaction of this present world for the future glory that is his in Christ. In contrast to the "buy now— pay later" attitude prevalent in the world, the Christian is willing to pay now and receive it later. What makes Christians willing to make such sacrifices? Hope, based on faith that the future holds something far better than the present. Paul writes in Romans 8:18, "I consider that the sufferings of this present time are not worthy to be compared with the glory that is to be revealed to us."*[6]

An eternal perspective acquired from God's Word is essential for any consistent and persevering Christian life. A great picture of this is offered in John Bunyan's classic allegory, *Pilgrim's Progress*. Bunyan's hero, Christian, had left his home like Abraham and started out on the way to eternal life. Along the way, he encountered one hardship after another. On one occasion he wandered off the path and got lost; later he was tempted by men named Simple, Sloth, and Presumption. Then he was wearied by the Hill of Difficulty, almost to be driven back by the roar of lions along the way.

Finally Christian came to the Castle Beautiful, a way station where he could rest and be equipped for the harrowing trials ahead. Many things he received there from godly helpers, and as he prepared to strike out again, they advised him to delay long enough to climb to a mountain from which he could gaze far, far ahead. Nestled in the Delectable Mountains was the Celestial City, the destination he sought. That vision alone gave vigor to his limbs and resolve to his heart.

Ahead of him lay many dangers and trials, spiritual warfare with Apollyon, persecution in the town of Vanity Fair, a harrowing escape through the Valley of the Shadow of Death. Yet that one vision of the city of heaven, the city with foundations, did much to encourage him forward through a long journey of trials.

That is how Abraham lived by faith for long years, in a land not his own. "He was looking forward to the city with foundations, whose architect and builder is God." If you are going to persevere in the Christian life, then you too must fix your eyes on that city. For that is your destination, that is your true home, although you know not what lies between it and you.

Like the apostle John in the Book of Revelation, you must by faith be taken away to "a mountain great and high," to see "the Holy City, Jerusalem, coming down out of heaven from God" (Rev. 21:10). It shines, we are told, "with the glory of God, and its brilliance was like that of a very precious jewel, like a jasper, clear as crystal" (Rev. 21:11). John tells us, "The city does not need the sun or the moon to shine on it, for the glory of God gives it light, and the Lamb is its lamp" (Rev. 21:23). There flows the river of the water of life, beside which grows the tree of life. John's vision concludes with these words:

> The leaves of the tree are for the healing of the nations. No longer will there be any curse. The throne of God and of the Lamb will be in the city, and his servants will serve him. They will see his face, and his name will be on their foreheads. There will be no more night. They will not need the light of a lamp or the light of the sun, for the Lord God will give them light. And they will reign for ever and ever. (Rev. 22:2–5)

That is the city to which you belong, if you have trusted in Christ, if you are trusting in him now. That is where this journey leads us, difficult though it is; by faith we shall some day arrive at the gates of the city with foundations, there to see the glory of God. There we shall find entry if these final words are true of us: "Blessed are those who wash their robes, that they may have the right to the tree of life and may go through the gates into the city" (Rev. 22:14).

That is where Christ leads us, through faith in him. That is the inheritance finally received after a life begun by faith responding to God's call, a life pursued by the receipt of God's promise, a life sustained by the vision of God's city yet to come. And if that is true—and it is—then surely we must live now as citizens belonging to there, as royal sons and daughters of heaven, where soon we shall be, with present hope and joy as we gladly serve our Savior and our God.

SIX

FAITH IN
THE PROMISE

HEBREWS 11:11-12

*By faith Abraham, even though he was past age—
and Sarah herself was barren—was enabled to become
a father because he considered him faithful who had made the
promise. And so from this one man, and he as good as dead,
came descendants as numerous as the stars in the sky and as
countless as the sand on the seashore. (Heb. 11:11–12)*

In this world you will have trouble." That is how our Lord
Jesus concluded his time with the disciples in the upper
room before heading out to the Garden of Gethsemane and
his arrest (John 16:33). Peter, who heard those words and
learned the truth of them, said in his first epistle, "Dear
friends, do not be surprised at the painful trial you are suffering, as though something strange were happening to you"
(1 Peter 4:12). This is something pastors learn quickly, that
there is much trouble and sorrow in the world. And every

one of us will learn and experience this if we live long enough.

That is important for us to realize when we are talking about faith, as does the eleventh chapter of Hebrews. Faith does not arise only in the soil of blessing or grow only when the sun is shining. Christian faith, at least, is not like faith in our favorite sports team, which blossoms only in the midst of a winning streak, or like faith in other people, which so easily withers when they let us down. What makes Christian faith so different is that its object is truly and always worthy of our trust. Our faith is in God, and even in sorrows and trials we are to say by faith, "The LORD is my strength and my song; he has become my salvation" (Ps. 118:14).

ABRAM'S GREAT SORROW

Our passage continues with the life of Abraham as an example of faith and brings to our attention what was surely the great sorrow of his life. Verse 11 says, "By faith Abraham, even though he was past age—and Sarah herself was barren—was enabled to become a father because he considered him faithful who had made the promise."

This verse refers to the situation, described beginning in Genesis 15, when God came to Abraham with a promise of great blessing: "Do not be afraid, Abram. I am your shield, your very great reward" (Gen 15:1). Imagine hearing such words from the Lord, and yet when Abram, as he then was called, heard them, instead of rejoicing he complained. "O Sovereign LORD," he said, "what can you give me since I remain childless and the one who will inherit my estate is Eliezer of Damascus? You have given me no children; so a servant in my household will be my heir" (Gen 15:2–3).

That scene encourages us that God does not dismiss us in anger when we complain to him, despite so many great blessings he provides. Abram here so resembles us. He is the beneficiary of amazing grace, and yet his heart is breaking because of the one thing dear to him that he does not have. The writer of Hebrews draws our attention to this circumstance to draw more lines on his portrait of the life of faith.

Abram's sorrow was made poignant by his name, which means "father of many." And yet he was into his later years and had not fathered a single child. Long before, God had promised, "To your offspring I will give this land" (Gen. 12:7), but after many years Abram had no offspring. This would be a source of great consternation in our society, but where Abram lived it was a galling humiliation. Donald Grey Barnhouse notes that Abram was a prominent man in a land that was a crossroads for travelers. He imagines a likely conversation with a merchant stopping by:

> In the evening time the merchants would have come to Abram's tent to pay their respects. The questions would have followed a set pattern. "How old are you? Who are you? How long have you been here?" When the trader had introduced himself, Abram would be forced to name himself: "Abram, father of many."
>
> It must have happened a hundred times, a thousand times, and each time more galling than the time before. "Oh, Father of many! Congratulations! And how many sons do you have?" And the answer was so humiliating to Abram: "None." And, many a time there must have been the half concealed snort of humor at the incongruity of the name and the fact that there were no children to back up such a name. Abram must have steeled himself for the ques-

tion and the reply, and have hated the situation with great bitterness.[1]

That is the way great sorrow and longing often rears its head. It sours otherwise pleasant encounters. Single people find it hard to be in married company, sometimes shying from the church for that reason. People like Abram and his wife, who cannot have children, often find the mere sound of children a constant reproach and burden. Men who think themselves failures cannot stand the success of others. Women who think themselves homely hate the beauty of those more blessed among their kind. On and on it goes, with life seeming like a parade of sadness and envy, heartbreak and discontent. However much we have, there is often a have-not that embitters our existence. We know, therefore, what it is like to be in Abram's shoes, responding to God's grace with an angry, teary cry: "What can you give me, since I have not this!"

The Bible responds to our cry of discontent directly, unabashedly making promises of great blessing. We find this in the case of Abram. Genesis 15 goes on to provide one of the most marvelous scenes in all of Scripture. First, God promised Abram a son from his body to be his heir. Abram had heard this before, and he was incredulous. Therefore, as he so often does, God appealed to another of Abram's senses, taking him outside under the canopy of stars, to which he led Abram's eyes. He said, "Look up at the heavens and count the stars—if indeed you can count them. . . . So shall your offspring be" (Gen. 15:5). Imagine the scene! We should let our imaginations dwell upon it—Abram being led by God out into the night to gaze upon the countless multitude of the stars in the dazzling desert sky as the measure of his coming blessing. How overwhelming it must have been; indeed, we know that it was overwhelming enough to overpower his un-belief. Genesis 15:6, the next verse, tells us Abram's re-sponse, which the apostle Paul uses as a paradigm for us all: "Abram believed the LORD, and he credited it to him as righ-teousness."

That is what this passage is about: faith in the promise of God. I want to consider it with three points: the God of prom-ises, the faith that waits, and the salvation that is all of grace.

THE GOD OF PROMISES

God relates to his children in this world largely through promises. If you look in the Old Testament you will find this is true. The Israelites were ever a people looking beyond the horizon, looking for the promise yet to come, yet to be ful-filled. That great coming arrived in the person in Jesus Christ, and yet Christians too are a people waiting for things that are yet to come. The New Testament believer looks for that which is promised and is yet to be fulfilled. As 2 Peter 1:4 says of God, "He has given us his very great and precious promises."

Abram's experience shows at least two reasons why God deals with us through promises. The first reason is to lift our eyes above the realm of our circumstances, even as he lifted Abram's eyes high into the heavens. All through our lives, God's promises lift our aspirations higher. On our own, we would be content with some happy relationships; God wants for us union with the Son of God. We aspire for earthly suc-cess; he intends for us heavenly glory. We would settle for health and wealth; he has in store life everlasting.

Such was the case with Abram. He wanted a son, but God intended that he would become the father of all the redeemed.

Already God had told Abram that through him he would bless all the nations (Gen. 12:3). But Abram's appetite was shaped, as ours so generally is, by his local and recent experience, by his felt needs, as they are called today. He wanted the caravan leaders to think highly of him. He wanted to know the human joy of looking into the eyes of a son. He wanted respect, he wanted to fit in, he wanted to feel good. These are things we want too. They are good things, so far as they go, but they fall far short of what God intends for us. Paul reminds us, "No eye has seen, no ear has heard, no mind has conceived what God has prepared for those who love him" (1 Cor. 2:9). To keep us from filling ourselves on lesser things, God leaves us in circumstances of want and gives us promises of great blessing, far beyond our imagining.

The second reason God deals with us through promises is related to the first and is also revealed in Abram's example. God is moving us along, calling us to our feet for a journey. Given a choice we would all settle down, here in this life, in this world, in this fleshly existence. Abram, we can be sure, would have been all too happy to raise a brood of sons alongside a good, clean well, with mud-baked bricks to form the walls of a sturdy house. But this is not our home; it is not where God would settle us forever. Again, Paul tells us, "For this world in its present form is passing away" (1 Cor. 7:31). We were not meant for this place, our souls were not created only for this life, and so God uses the combination of want and promises to raise us to our feet and move us along the way.

When we realize that God deals with us through promises and when we start looking for them, we soon begin to feel like Abram out beneath the starry host. The promises of God are great beyond all reckoning. J. C. Ryle puts it well:

There are "shalls" and "wills" in God's treasury for every condition. About God's infinite mercy and compassion; about His readiness to receive all who repent and believe; about His willingness to forgive, pardon and absolve the chief of sinners; about His power to change hearts and alter our corrupt nature; about the encouragements to pray and hear the gospel and draw near to the throne of grace; about strength for duty, comfort in trouble, guidance in perplexity, help in sickness, consolation in death, support under bereavement, happiness beyond the grave, reward in glory—about all these things there is an abundant supply of promises in the Word. No one can form an idea of its abundance unless he carefully searches the Scriptures, keeping the subject steadily in view. If anyone doubts it, I can only say, "Come and see." Like the Queen of Sheba at Solomon's court, you will soon say, "The half was not told me" (1 Ki. 10:7).[2]

THE FAITH THAT WAITS

Abram received God's great promise with faith, and yet the years to come proved nonetheless hard. His wife particularly seems to have suffered from her inability to bear children. In Genesis 16:1–2 we see how she responded:

> Now Sarai, Abram's wife, had borne him no children. But she had an Egyptian maidservant named Hagar; so she said to Abram, "The LORD has kept me from having children. Go, sleep with my maidservant; perhaps I can build a family through her."

Abram slept with Hagar, and she conceived, bearing him a son named Ishmael. This may have seemed an answer to prayer, a blessing from God, but if so the delusion was soon dispelled. The first result was turmoil within Abram's house, as Hagar and Sarai predictably launched a bitter war for pride of place and authority. That took place when Abram was eighty-six years old, ten years after his arrival in the land. The second problem revealed itself thirteen years later, when Abram was ninety-nine, when God came to him to reaffirm the original promise and inform him that Ishmael would not be the son of blessing.

The problem with Sarai's suggestion and Abram's action was that they tried to achieve God's promise by human power. Abram had grown weary over so many years, and his wife's discouragement wore away at his resolve. Finally he gave up on the idea of such an elderly woman bearing a child—something humanly impossible—and decided to help things along by taking Hagar to his bed.

That is the kind of thing we are tempted to do. We have a great longing and trust that God intends to bless us according to his wisdom. But to help him out we take matters into our hands, according to our wisdom, even employing sinful means to attain the ends we want. Tired of waiting for a husband, we give in to premarital sex in order to win a man's heart. Anxious to get that promotion we so richly deserve, we lie or take advantage of other people in a way dishonoring to God. We justify all this by faith, just as Abram and Sarai must have done, when in fact it is unbelief that is holding our hands. Doubting God's power for what seems impossible, we manipulate what is possible by our devices.

This happens in churches too. Eager to do God's work but unwilling to wait on his timetable, many churches go about it in human ways. Thus we use psychological manipulation to create the appearance of conversions, when in fact only God can convert the soul. Eager to fill the church—surely God wants that—we resort to cheap marketing and other patently unbiblical measures. Although God says his Word is sufficient for all our needs, churches all too easily cast Sarah aside for the seemingly more fertile embrace of Hagar. Whenever churches do that, they, like Abram, bear illegitimate children who, like Ishmael, are denied the blessing of God.

Genesis 17 tells us of God's return to Abram, when Ishmael was thirteen years old. God challenged him, even while renewing the promise. He said, "I am God Almighty; walk before me and be blameless. I will confirm my covenant between me and you and will greatly increase your numbers" (vv. 1–2). Clearly God was confronting Abram for his unbelief and sin. "I am God Almighty," he said, forcefully asserting his worthiness to be trusted absolutely, his omnipotent power to accomplish all he had promised. "Walk before me and be blameless," he then commanded, pressing forth his requirement of obedience. Rebuking Abram's unbelief and encouraging him to new faith, God added, "I will confirm my covenant . . . and will greatly increase your numbers."

Abram was ninety-nine years old, but his success with Hagar showed that he could produce children. Therefore it must have been a great encouragement to Abram, however astounding it might have been, when God declared that henceforth his name would be Abraham. Not Abram, father of many, but Abraham, father of a people. Surely God intended this to be a sign to the world of Abram's faith in him. Abram had stumbled in his faith, but God placed him back upon his feet with an even greater sign of blessing and a call to renewed trust.

Imagine aged Abram coming back from this meeting, setting his one child beside him and announcing that he had a new name. People would have whispered, "He finally couldn't take it any more. It's going to be Abechad, 'father of one.'" How astonished they must have been when the man of faith announced, "My name is no longer Abram, father of many, but Abraham, father of a nation." That was the kind of absolute conviction and commitment that God demanded of Abraham, and he demands it of us as well.

The point is that faith must wait upon the Lord. Abram was seventy-five years old when he set out for Canaan, eighty-six when he gave in and had a child with Hagar, and ninety-nine when God set him back on his feet with the renewed promise and change of name. Faith receives God's promise and faith waits on him, often for long periods.

The psalms constantly extol this theme. Psalm 27 ends, "Wait for the LORD; be strong and take heart and wait for the LORD" (v. 14). Psalm 37 says, "Be still before the LORD and wait patiently for him. . . . Wait for the LORD and keep his way" (vv. 7, 34). Psalm 130 puts it in words perhaps closest to our hearts: "I wait for the LORD, my soul waits, and in his word I put my hope. My soul waits for the Lord more than watchmen wait for the morning, more than watchmen wait for the morning" (vv. 5–6). Charles Haddon Spurgeon comments, "This is a most divine precept, and requires much grace to carry it out. To hush the spirit, to be silent before the Lord, to wait in holy patience the time for clearing up the difficulties of Providence—this is what every gracious heart should aim at." Waiting on the Lord is difficult, but it is the sign of a wise and believing heart that trusts an omnipotent and gracious God. Spurgeon concludes, "Time is nothing to him, let it be nothing to thee. God is worth waiting for. . . . Wait in obedience as a servant, in hope as an heir, in expectation as a believer."[3]

To wait upon the Lord is to rely on him; it is to study and trust his attributes. It is, for instance, to know that he is faithful, often in ways we had never considered before. It involves committing ourselves to his power, to his goodness, to his wisdom, as all of these unite to superintend the affairs of our lives, not according to our plan but according to his. These are the things the psalms talk about as they exhort us to wait upon the Lord. Psalm 27 begins with words of comfort, based on who and what God is: "The LORD is my light and my salvation—whom shall I fear? The LORD is the stronghold of my life—of whom shall I be afraid?" (v. 1).

Faith waits upon the Lord. A. W. Pink says this:

> *Faith provides a firm standing-ground while I await the fulfillment of God's promises. Faith furnishes my heart with a sure support during the interval. Faith believes God and relies upon His veracity: as it does so, the heart is anchored and remains steady, no matter how fierce the storm nor how protracted the season of waiting. . . . Real faith issues in a confident and standing expectation of future things.*[4]

Despite stumbling into unbelief and sin, Abraham sets for us a great example of waiting on the Lord in faith. Our text rightly says of him, "By faith Abraham, even though he was past age—and Sarah herself was barren—was enabled to become a father because he considered him faithful who had made the promise." Romans 4:20–21 gives another description of this waiting faith, a classic statement of what faith is all about. Speaking of Abraham, Paul writes, "He did not waver through unbelief regarding the promise of God, but was strengthened in his faith and gave glory to God, being fully persuaded that God had power to do what he had promised."

ALL OF GRACE

Our passage in Hebrews 11 seems to have a specific episode in mind, because it includes for us Sarah's faith that also received the promise. Indeed, there is some question as to who is the main subject of verse 11, Abraham or Sarah. I think the flow of thought makes him the main subject, as it clearly leads to Abraham in verse 12. Yet it was together that this sorrowful pair found grace to trust in God and in his promise.

Abraham was ninety-nine when God renewed the promise, and yet he did not have the child of promise. God had changed his name, and he also changed the name of his wife, from Sarai to Sarah, a name that means "princess," to indicate that his promise still dealt with her. Yes, Abraham would father a nation, but not through young slave girls he purchased and brought to his bed. It would be through his legitimate wife, Sarah, despite her advanced age and barren womb. In Genesis 17:15–16 God said this: "As for Sarai your wife, you are no longer to call her Sarai; her name will be Sarah. I will bless her and will surely give you a son by her. I will bless her so that she will be the mother of nations; kings of peoples will come from her."

God's insistence that Abraham's offspring be born through Sarah is a sign that salvation is by grace alone. God has promised great blessing to Abraham in terms of offspring. We have talked about the embarrassment he suffered in going so long without children, but there is another matter that is far more significant. Abraham's childlessness brought God's covenant into question, God's faithfulness and his plan of salvation. How would the world be blessed, how would the seed of salvation come? Would it be by natural means, by works, or by supernatural means, by grace alone? We find God's plain answer in his promise regarding Sarah. "She will be the mother of nations," God said of this ninety-year-old, wrinkled woman. "Kings of peoples will come from her."

On the surface, this is laughable. In fact, Abraham did laugh at this idea. The next verses, Genesis 16:17–20, tell us, "Abraham fell facedown; he laughed and said to himself, 'Will a son be born to a man a hundred years old? Will Sarah bear a child at the age of ninety?' . . . Then God said, 'Yes, but your wife Sarah will bear you a son, and you will call him Isaac. I will establish my covenant with him as an everlasting covenant for his descendants after him.'"

That is how God has designed salvation to work, in a manner that confounds human expectation and leaves all the glory to him alone. In Genesis 18 God makes the same promise again, this time in the presence of Sarah, and she laughed too (Gen. 18:12). But Genesis 21 tells us that Abraham went to her, and she did have a son. They named him Isaac, which means "laughter," no longer laughing tears of unbelief but tears of joy and renewed wonder at the power and faithfulness of the promise-keeping God.

Hebrews 11:12 speaks of this, telling us what can happen when faith waits upon God's promise: "And so from this one man, and he as good as dead, came descendants as numerous as the stars in the sky and as countless as the sand on the seashore." Fighting through their natural tendency to unbelief, Abraham and Sarah did trust the Lord. I think it is wonderful that Hebrews 11 says nothing about their unbelieving laughter and complaints, sins that were washed away by the blood of Christ, but only about their faith, which God remembered. Believing God, they came together as husband and wife, and by the power of his grace God brought life from the dead womb, bringing about a salvation that is all of grace.

In that manner, the barren womb signifies salvation by grace all through the Bible. Isaiah could boldly write, "Sing, O barren woman, you who never bore a child; burst into song, shout for joy, you who were never in labor; because more are the children of the desolate woman than of her who has a husband" (Isa. 54:1).

All this rose to a new level when another descendant of Abraham, indeed his special seed God had in mind all along, was born not of the barren but of the virgin womb. The barren womb speaks of human failure and weakness and futility; the virgin womb speaks of a work that belongs to God alone, in which human works have no place at all, a rock cut not with human hands. God spoke to Joseph about a child from his virgin fiancée's womb: "She will give birth to a son, and you are to give him the name Jesus, because he will save his people from their sins" (Matt. 1:21).

The virgin birth tells us that the means by which the gospel produces its ends are not natural, are not humanly controlled, are not something we can manipulate for our success or that rely upon us. The blessing God promised to Abraham could come about only if a barren and elderly woman could conceive and give birth. When it comes to Christ we find that there will be salvation from our sins only if a virgin girl can do the same. That Sarah conceived and gave birth, that Mary did the same, tells us that the salvation we trust is of God from first to last and to the glory of his name alone. Let us therefore trust ourselves to this God who gives life to the dead and produces blessing from the barren womb, even salvation through the virgin womb from which came our Lord Jesus Christ.

Surely this exhorts us to turn to God for the whole of our need and with all of our longings, trusting his might and waiting upon him for all the precious promises we receive in Scripture. Jeremiah Burroughs thus exhorts us: "Every time a godly man reads the Scriptures . . . and there meets with a promise, he ought to lay his hand upon it and say, This is part of my inheritance, it is mine, and I am to live upon it."[5]

Then let us realize that the greatest of all our inheritance is God; his greatest promise is this: "I will be your God and you will be my people." It is God we receive as we rest upon his promises. And it is our hearts that he is seeking through this long and sometimes difficult life of faith as he calls us to wait upon him. Through the faith of Abraham we too may receive the words of blessing God gave to him, "Do not be afraid. I am your shield, your very great reward" (Gen. 15:1).

SEVEN

FAITH SEEKING
A HOME

HEBREWS 11:13–16

*All these people were still living by faith when
they died. They did not receive the things promised; they
only saw them and welcomed them from a distance. And they
admitted that they were aliens and strangers on earth. People
who say such things show that they are looking for a country of
their own. If they had been thinking of the country they had left,
they would have had opportunity to return. Instead, they were
longing for a better country—a heavenly one. Therefore
God is not ashamed to be called their God, for he has
prepared a city for them. (Heb. 11:13–16)*

The apostle Paul illustrated his teaching on the doctrine of
justification by faith by appealing to the example of Abraham. In Romans 4:11–12, Paul points out that Abraham is
the father of believing Jews and believing Gentiles in their
faith. He writes this:

He is the father of all who believe but have not been circum-
cised, in order that righteousness might be credited to them.
And he is also the father of the circumcised who not only are
circumcised but who also walk in the footsteps of the faith
that our father Abraham had before he was circumcised.

Paul's point is that neither circumcision nor uncircumci-
sion matters, for Abraham was justified by faith alone before he
was circumcised. What matters is walking in the footsteps of
faith, footsteps laid out before us by our father in faith, Abraham. That kind of statement makes our studies of the faith of
Abraham something more than academic. If we are saved, he is
our father in faith, and the steps he walked we are to walk behind him. John Murray, in his commentary on Romans, says,
"To 'walk in the footsteps' is to march in file. Abraham is conceived of as the leader of the band and we walk, not abreast, but
in file, following in the footsteps left by Abraham."[1]

Many people tend think of the Christian life only in terms
of a past, definitive event. We talk about having been born
again or deciding for Jesus as if that were the whole of the
Christian life. But the idea of walking in faith shows us that
the Christian life is a pilgrimage with its destination not in
this life at all but only far off in the next. That is what our passage explores as we continue to study Abraham's faith. It
presents us with three points: the end of faith's journey, faith
leaving its worldly home, and faith seeking a true and heavenly home with God.

THE END OF FAITH'S JOURNEY

The verses before us look upon faith as a pilgrimage and
begin by describing what the end of this life's journey looks

like for a Christian. "All these people were still living by faith when they died. They did not receive the things promised; they only saw them and welcomed them from a distance" (Heb. 11:13).

It is not certain whether "all these people" refers to all the examples given from the beginning of Hebrews 11 or to Abraham and his immediate family. The context suggests only the latter, although these words could be said of every believer presented in the Bible. They died still believing but not having all the things their faith set itself upon. They were looking for something not realized in this world, in this life. The promises they trusted were not fulfilled in their present earthly existence: "They only saw them and welcomed them from afar." Abraham was promised children, and he did live to see the promised son from the womb of Sarah. But all that God had promised, offspring like stars in the sky and with them his possession of the land, did not occur in his earthly life. He died still hoping for all that he had longed for and sojourned toward in this life.

This verse might seem to express a tragedy. After all, Abraham and those with him spent their whole lives longing for things they were promised, longing to have a home of their own; they trusted God for this and believed the promises he gave them, and yet they died without having received them. What a dismal story! What a poor commendation for the faith they represented! If this is what our faith is about, dying with only unfulfilled hopes, then surely we are, as Paul said, "to be pitied more than all men" (1 Cor. 15:19).

One thing this tells us, however, is that Christianity is not a religion focused on the earth and this present life. The Scriptures make this point over and over. Paul says in Colossians 3:2, "Set your minds on things above, not on earthly things." Jesus taught, "Do not store up for yourselves trea-sures on earth, where moth and rust destroy, and where thieves break in and steal. But store up for yourselves trea-sures in heaven, where moth and rust do not destroy, and where thieves do not break in and steal" (Matt. 6:19–20).

This directly confronts a view that is prevalent in our time, a packaged version of Christianity that offers mainly temporal benefits. It goes like this: "If you trust Jesus, you will do better at work, you will be a better husband or wife or parent, you will have less stress and lose weight." Christian-ity does give us spiritual resources that transform this present life, like righteousness, peace, and joy. But how easily we for-get that to be a Christian means to be persecuted in this world. Our blessings are spiritual rather than material (see Eph. 1:3). It means living as an alien and a pilgrim, it means not being able to fit in with others who are slaves to sin, it means denying yourself and picking up your cross, it means a life of struggle and of fellowship in the sufferings of Christ. It means peace with God but war with the flesh, the world, and the devil. The primary blessings Christianity offers do not lie in this life but in the life to come, in the resurrection from the dead. Indeed, even our present blessings, abundant and won-derful as they are, are located there and are accessed by the exercise of faith.

It never crossed the apostle Paul's mind that to be a Christian meant happiness and health and wealth in this present life. Instead, he admitted that if we do not receive great blessings beyond the grave, we would be better off living like hedonists, enjoying the temporary pleasures of sin. "If the dead are not raised," he argued, " 'Let us eat and drink, for tomorrow we die' " (1 Cor. 15:32).

That is essentially how the world lives, but it is not the

way of Christians. Christians realize that even at the end of this life, the blessings we have hoped for will not yet have been received. We are pilgrims here, and our homeland, our rest, our treasure lies in the land across the grave. Hebrews 11:13 says, "They did not receive the things promised; they only saw them and welcomed them from a distance." Christians are presently filled with joy because of the certainty of what lies ahead; by faith we greet and enjoy the things promised for the life to come.

It is obvious, therefore, that the Christian has a vastly different view of death than does the non-Christian. I mentioned the apostle Paul's emphasis on the life to come; that emphasis greatly shaped his view of death. He wrote his letter to the Philippians from a Roman jail, fully aware that he might be put to death. His attitude to all this was wonderfully straightforward: "For to me, to live is Christ and to die is gain" (Phil. 1:21). He lived in this world as a servant of Christ, with a longing for Christ, and therefore death became the means by which his heart's desire could be achieved. Paul was not suicidal; he was willing to live as long as the Lord intended for him. But far from fearing death, he saw it as the crowning moment of his faith.

Some years later Paul was back in jail for preaching the gospel, this time sure that death loomed. He wrote to Timothy, "I have fought the good fight, I have finished the race, I have kept the faith. Now there is in store for me the crown of righteousness, which the Lord, the righteous Judge, will award to me on that day" (2 Tim. 4:7–8). Paul was not like the man of this world, who faces death looking backwards, thinking about the good old days, about his glorious achievements, and wishing he could go back. For Paul all this life was but a journey to what lies beyond death, a crown of righteousness and a home in glory with the Lord. No matter how full this life might have been, it was merely preparation for what is yet to come. In contrast to whatever wonders one might have experienced here, Paul could say, "No eye has seen, no ear has heard, no mind has conceived what God has prepared for those who love him" (1 Cor. 2:9).

Paul's view of death was centered on the cross of Jesus Christ. It is because of the cross that Paul could say in 1 Corinthians 15:54–55, " 'Death has been swallowed up in victory.' 'Where, O death, is your victory? Where, O death, is your sting?' " This does not mean that death is no longer terrible, that it is no longer an enemy. It is an enemy, but one that Christ has vanquished by taking from us the guilt of our sin. This is what the next verses say: "The sting of death is sin, and the power of sin is the law. But thanks be to God! He gives us the victory through our Lord Jesus Christ" (1 Cor. 15:56–57).

The Westminster Shorter Catechism summarizes the Bible's teaching on what death does for a believer: "The souls of believers are at their death made perfect in holiness, and do immediately pass into glory, and their bodies, being still united to Christ, do rest in their graves till the resurrection" (Q/A 37). Thomas Watson writes:

> A believer at death is freed from sin; he is not taken away in, but from his sins; he shall never have a vain, proud thought more; he shall never grieve the Spirit of God any more. . . . Death smites a believer as the angel did Peter, and made his chains fall off (Acts 12:7). Believers at death are made perfect in holiness. . . . Oh! what a blessed privilege is this, to be without spot or wrinkle; to be purer than the sunbeams; to be as free from sin as the angels!

(Eph. 5:27). This makes a believer desirous to have his passport and to be gone; he would fain live in that pure air where no black vapours of sin arise.[2]

Our verse says that Abraham and the others "were still living by faith when they died," and what a difference that makes for every child of God in the hour of death, which, unless the Lord should come, all of us must someday face. Charles Haddon Spurgeon says this:

> *The grave—what is it? It is the bath in which the Christian puts on the clothes of his body to have them washed and cleansed. Death—what is it? It is the waiting room where we robe ourselves for immortality; it is the place where the body, like Esther, bathes itself in spices that it may be fit for the embrace of its Lord. Death is the gate of life; I will not fear to die, then.*[3]

Abraham's approach to death is instructive for us. We see here that he never did receive the promise of owning the land during his life. Genesis 23, however, tells us what he did when the time came to prepare for death. Sarah, his wife, finally died at a great old age, and Abraham mourned and wept over her. But then he did something he had never done before. He went to Ephron the Hittite, a nearby landowner, and bought a piece of land, the cave of Machpelah, as the burial place for Sarah and later for himself. Abraham was obviously well respected, because Ephron wanted to give him the land without making him pay. But Abraham insisted; he would own that one piece of Canaan outright. You see the point Abraham was making: In life he was a pilgrim on that land, but in death he would be an owner. His and Sarah's bodies would lie on land owned by him, because it was in death that he looked for the fulfillment of God's promise of a land and a home.

Abraham died in the faith. Spurgeon thinks on this and sees in his mind a mausoleum erected by God, not unlike Abraham's cave, in which lie the bodies of all his people. On it, he sees inscribed the words of Hebrews 11:13: "These all died in faith." He writes, "As for those who died without faith, they died indeed; but, as for his people, a glorious resurrection awaits them. They sleep in Jesus, and are blest, how kind their slumbers are."[4]

FAITH LEAVING A HOME

Our passage describes the life of faith as a pilgrimage in a foreign land, a journey through life to a home that awaits beyond the grave. Verses 13–15 make an important point about such a pilgrimage, namely, that it requires that we first leave our prior home: "They admitted that they were aliens and strangers on earth. People who say such things show that they are looking for a country of their own. If they had been thinking of the country they had left, they would have had opportunity to return."

Abraham and the others confessed themselves to be aliens and strangers. This is a direct quote from Genesis 23:4. When Abraham went to the Hittites to buy his burial plot, he told them, "I am an alien and a stranger among you." In the Greek, the writer of Hebrews renders this with two words, the first of which is *xenoi*, meaning "aliens." This was a pejorative term indicating outsiders. It is not the sort of word one wanted to have applied to himself. It describes not merely a person from another place but rather someone who doesn't fit in, who doesn't belong. In our society, aliens can assimilate, but the writer of Hebrews says that in this world Christians never do.

The other term is *parepidemoi*, or "sojourners." These are ones who are passing through to a destination somewhere else. In Greek writings the term was applied to someone lodging temporarily in an inn, without a home in the place where he found himself even if he would be there a while. That is what our text says about Abraham and those who follow him in faith. By admitting they are aliens and strangers they "show that they are looking for a country of their own" (v. 14).

Since we all come from someplace, this requires the believer to leave home to answer God's call. Abraham was living in the land of his fathers when God called him to leave and go to the land of promise, there to live as an alien and a stranger. Hebrews commends him for his faith in that he made no attempt to go back: "If they had been thinking of the country they had left, they would have had opportunity to return." Nothing stood between Abraham and his former home, nothing except his faith. The fact that he made no attempt to go back shows the strength and reality of that faith.

Practically the worst thing that can be said of someone who once has professed faith in Christ is that he went back to the home he had left. Lot's wife was turned into a pillar of salt because she looked back on Sodom; her heart went back with her eyes, and for this God judged her for unbelief. The strongest charge laid against the Israelites in the exodus was that they complained about the hardships of their journey and longed to return to their former slavery in Egypt. Numbers 11:4–5 tells us, "The Israelites started wailing and said, 'If only we had meat to eat! We remember the fish we ate in Egypt at no cost—also the cucumbers, melons, leeks, onions and garlic.' " For that and other sins God made a whole generation wander and die in the desert. It was for the same spiritual betrayal that Paul sadly reported the apostasy of one of his helpers: "Demas, because he loved this world, has deserted me" (2 Tim. 4:10). In contrast to those examples, people of faith are like Peter and James and John when Jesus called them to follow. Luke 5:11 tells us, "They pulled their boats up on the shore, left everything and followed him."

Whether or not we have really left this world, the place of our former allegiance, is determined not just by what we say but by how we live. This seems to have been a teaching greatly stressed in the early church. One very early document, the *Epistle to Diognetus*, speaks of this subject in strong terms: "[Christians] dwell in their own countries, but only as sojourners. . . . Every foreign country is a homeland to them, and every homeland is foreign. . . . Their existence is on earth, but their citizenship is in heaven."[5] Jesus put this as a simple challenge: "Where your treasure is, there your heart will be also" (Matt. 6:21). And where your heart is, surely that is your home.

Abraham left Ur and no longer thought of himself in terms of his former home but of the home to which he was headed. Let me ask you, then, if that is true of you. In what terms do you think of yourself? What is it that provides your identity? Is it your family background? Is it your race or social class or profession? Is it your earthly homeland or the school from which you graduated? If these are the sources of your identity and your thinking and your desires, then they are still your home. You have not set your heart upon the city that is to come, the heavenly home to which God has called you. Your old allegiances will hold you back and discourage you from a true pilgrimage in faith before the Lord. This does not mean that Christians must physically change their place of residence, although that might be involved, but rather we must exchange our former hopes and dreams and affections in this world for new ones in Christ and in the world to come.

Christians are to increasingly think of themselves not in terms of the old categories, the old homeland, but in terms of where we are headed, in terms of him who calls us and those with whom we will spend eternity in heaven. What liberty it gives us for godliness when our hearts have left our earthly homes! What an ally in repudiating worldliness and sin and in putting on a heavenly character! If we will not leave behind our former home, we cannot advance to the heavenly place God has called us; if we will not leave, we show that we are not longing for a better country, a heavenly one. This is a sober test of our faith, as Jesus put it:

> Anyone who loves his father or mother more than me is not worthy of me; anyone who loves his son or daughter more than me is not worthy of me; and anyone who does not take his cross and follow me is not worthy of me. Whoever finds his life will lose it, and whoever loses his life for my sake will find it. (Matt. 10:37–39)

FAITH SEEKING A HOME

Abraham willingly left everything, and in this he shows us what faith requires. Faith leaves one home in search of another. "They were longing for a better country—a heavenly one," says verse 16. This is not only the counterpart to the idea of living as a stranger and an alien, but it is the rationale and motive. What is it that makes people spend their lives as those passing through except that they are headed somewhere dear to their hearts? Abraham lived as a pilgrim here because of his eagerness to have that which can be possessed only by faith and is achieved only in a world that is yet to come. His home was elsewhere, with God and the city God had prepared, and so it was only natural for him to live the way he did.

Let me put this differently. We saw earlier how Christians view the matter of death. Death itself is terrible. Death itself is not a good thing. But for those who trust the Lord it becomes the gateway into life. If we believe that, then our view of death will change our view of life. It is not here that we will set our hearts, but there beyond life's horizon. This new focus transforms our view of present trials and sorrows. A famous preacher expressed this attitude in a letter to a friend announcing the death of his dear beloved wife:

> I have some of the best news to impart. One beloved by you has accomplished her warfare, has received an answer to her prayers, and everlasting joy rests upon her head. My dear wife, the source of my best earthly comfort for twenty years, departed on Tuesday.[6]

It is not that this man felt no sadness at the loss of his wife, but he understood what death meant for her. It meant finding and reaching the home and joy for which she long had sought. Christians by faith have seen better things in another place. Our treasure is there, and so our heart follows. Therefore we gladly accept the fact that we are sojourners here, because that tells us we have an inheritance there; as the well-loved hymn puts it, we will "cherish the old rugged cross, and exchange it someday for a crown."

Armed with this attitude, Christians do not settle down

here, do not settle for lesser riches. This is what John Bunyan conveyed in *Pilgrim's Progress*, when Christian explained his departure to those who tried to keep him from leaving his home, puzzled by his eagerness to depart a comfortable worldly life. Christian explained, urging them to come with him:

> *Everything you forsake is not worthy of being compared with what I am seeking to enjoy (2 Cor. 4:18). If you will come with me, and hold steady, we will prosper. For where I go, there is enough and to spare (Lk. 15:17). Come with me, and prove my words.*

One of the men replied:

> *What are the things you seek, since you leave all the world to find them?*

Christian answered:

> *I seek an inheritance incorruptible, undefiled, that does not fade away (1 Pet. 1:4). It is reserved and safe in heaven (Heb. 11:16), to be given at the time appointed to them that diligently seek it.[7]*

Such a one was Abraham. His faith too sought a home, a heavenly city God had prepared for him. Every Christian knows something of that yearning Abraham knew, living in tents in sight of the earthly city, looking upon its pleasures but lifting his eyes to the promises of God, forsaking the one so as to gain the other.

How wonderful, then, to read what verse 16 says in conclusion: "Therefore God is not ashamed to be called their

God, for he has prepared a city for them." What could be more lovely than this: that God, the holy God and the God of grace, the sovereign God of all the world, is not ashamed of them that trust in him, that sojourn in this world longing for the home he has prepared? What Jesus said to the woman by the well is surely true of Abraham and all who walk in his steps: "They are the kind of worshipers the Father seeks" (John 4:23).

All those long years Abraham identified himself not by the home he had left, not by the place where he resided, but by the home he was seeking and by the God who called him and gave the promises he believed. He and his sons were willing to be called men of God, not men of the world, and therefore God was willing to say, as we so often read in the Old Testament: "I am the God of Abraham, the God of Isaac and the God of Jacob" (Exod. 3:6). If we would walk in Abraham's steps then we may insert our names in that place. God eagerly says to us, "I will be your God, and you will be my people." To all who will hear he unashamedly says of us, "I am their God," if in return we will say to the world that we are his.

TWO DEATHS

Our passage speaks about dying in faith and receiving a home in place of the one we have left in this passing world. What a difference it makes in the hour of death to have a better home beyond the grave, a country and a city prepared for us by God! But what a tragedy death is for all whose only home is here, who have no home and no life except in this poor and dying world.

In 1899 two prominent men died, and the manner of their deaths well illustrates this difference. The first was

Colonel Robert G. Ingersoll, for whom the Ingersoll lectures on immortality at Harvard University are named, and who gave his brilliant mind to the refutation of Christianity. Ingersoll died suddenly that year, leaving his unprepared family devastated. So grief-stricken was his wife that she would not allow his body to be taken from their home until the health of the family required its removal. His remains then were cremated, and his funeral service was such a scene of dismay and despair that even the newspapers of the day commented upon it. Death came to this man, and there was no hope but only an irredeemable tragedy.

The other man who died that year was Dwight L. Moody, the great Christian evangelist. He had been declining for some time, and his family had gathered around his bed. On his last morning, his son heard him exclaim, "Earth is receding; heaven is opening; God is calling." "You are dreaming, Father," said his son. But Moody replied, "No, Will, this is no dream. I have been within the gates. I have seen the children's faces." Moody seemed to revive but then started to slip away again. "Is this death?" he was heard to say. "This is not bad; there is no valley. This is bliss. This is glorious." His daughter had come, and she began to pray for him to recover. "No, no, Emma," he said. "Don't pray for that. God is calling. This is my coronation day. I have been looking forward to it."

Moody died not long after that, his family confident of his entry into heaven. His funeral was a scene of triumph and great joy. Those in attendance sang hymns and exalted God. "Where, O death, is your victory? Where, O death, is your sting?" they exclaimed. Walking in Abraham's steps, the Christian had found the home he had been seeking for all his earthly sojourn. He had not been ashamed of God, and now God was not ashamed of him. He had lived for God in this world, leaving behind its pleasures and its glory, and God had prepared a city for him, "an inheritance," Peter says, "that can never perish, spoil or fade—kept in heaven" for him (1 Peter 1:4). "Now," he could say along with Paul, "there is in store for me the crown of righteousness, which the Lord, the righteous Judge, will award to me on that day—and not only to me, but also to all who have longed for his appearing" (2 Tim. 4:8).

EIGHT

FAITH TESTED

HEBREWS 11:17–19

*By faith Abraham, when God tested him, offered
Isaac as a sacrifice. He who had received the promises was
about to sacrifice his one and only son, even though God had
said to him, "It is through Isaac that your offspring will be reckoned." Abraham reasoned that God could raise the dead,
and figuratively speaking, he did receive Isaac
back from death. (Heb. 11:17–19)*

In the twenty-second chapter of Genesis, we read that God
came to Abraham and tested him. It marks the fifth time
that Genesis deliberately records God appearing to Abraham.
The first occurred in Genesis 12, God's initial call to Abraham. In Genesis 15, God came and promised Abraham descendants like stars in the sky. In Genesis 17, God came to
redirect Abraham to the path of faith he had departed in his
encounter with Hagar. In Genesis 18, the angel of the Lord
appeared to Sarah and him to announce the birth of the child
of promise and to deal with the problem of sin in Sodom and

Gomorrah. In the first of these, God called Abraham to faith; in the second and third encounters God strengthened his faith; in the fourth encounter God rewarded his faith. Now, in the fifth and last of these significant encounters between Abraham and the Lord, that faith would be tested by the most difficult of commands.

The New Testament confirms that God tests the faith of his people. In 1 Peter, the apostle speaks of various trials and then adds, "These have come so that your faith—of greater worth than gold, which perishes even though refined by fire—may be proved genuine and may result in praise, glory and honor when Jesus Christ is revealed" (1 Peter 1:7). The purpose is the strengthening of faith by trial, the proving of faith by means of tests God provides.

ABRAHAM'S FAITH TESTED

God tested Abraham with the greatest trial imaginable. Genesis 22:2 tells us, "Then God said, 'Take your son, your only son, Isaac, whom you love, and go to the region of Moriah. Sacrifice him there as a burnt offering on one of the mountains.' "

First, this was a trial of Abraham's devotion to the Lord. Devotion to God is at the heart of his law: "Love the LORD your God with all your heart and with all your soul and with all your strength" (Deut. 6:5). The proof of love is always found in the willingness to sacrifice. God tested Abraham not merely by asking a sacrifice, or even a great sacrifice, but the sacrifice of that which Abraham held most dear, his covenant heir, Isaac. The test of our Christian devotion always involves this, that we love not so much the gifts—great as they are— but the Giver above all. The question is always whether we are willing to make God first; indeed, whether we are willing to make him everything. John Owen writes:

> God says to us, "My son, give me your heart" (Prov. 23:26). And God commands us to love him with all our heart, soul, strength and mind (Lk. 10:27). This is the response God wants from us in return for his love to us. . . . This is love, that God loves us first, and then we love him in response to his love.[1]

We might wonder if God has the right to demand such singular devotion. The answer is a resounding yes! A. W. Pink explains:

> The Lord has an absolute claim upon us, upon all that we have. As our Maker and Sovereign He has the right to demand from us anything He pleases, and whatsoever He requires we must yield. All that we have comes from Him, and must be held for Him, and at His disposal. . . . The bounty of God should encourage us to surrender freely whatever He calls for, for none ever lose by giving up anything to God.[2]

We can expect God to test our devotion to him, in great or small ways. We will be challenged to sacrifice or subordinate our careers to his will. Or perhaps it will be a relationship that is dear to us but that cannot abide with our higher devotion to Jesus Christ. It may be money; it may be a certain self-image or a lifestyle; it can be practically anything. God tests our faith in terms of our willingness to sacrifice for him, and in this manner he also protects us from the idolatry to which our hearts are so unfailingly prone. Even good things he has given us, such as Isaac, this child of God's promise, God demands that we place back into his hand, always holding everything as a trust on behalf of the Giver and Possessor of all things.

Second, this was a trial of Abraham's spiritual understanding. We see this in verses 17–18: "He who had received the promises was about to sacrifice his one and only son, even though God had said to him, 'It is through Isaac that your offspring will be reckoned.'" God had made great and surpassing promises to Abraham—possession of the land, offspring like the sands on the seashore, all the nations blessed through him—all to be fulfilled through this son, Isaac, whom God now commanded him to sacrifice.

We can see how vexing this would have been. God's promise seemed to have been pitted against God's command. If God was to be faithful to his promises to Abraham, then Isaac must live; but if God's command was to be obeyed, then Isaac must die. It seemed to have been so inconsistent, so internally contradictory. None of us is likely to get this particular command from God, but God may call us to obey him in a way that seems spiritually counterproductive to ourselves or our projects, and like Abraham we will have to summon up the spiritual understanding needed to obey God's Word.

Third, it was a trial of Abraham's knowledge of God and trust in him. I say this because of the horror of what was involved in this command. Abraham was to strike his son dead. Furthermore, it was "his one and only son." This was not strictly speaking true, for Isaac was not the only living son; the point is that he was the one child of the promise, the one heir of the covenant. William L. Lane writes, "When Abraham obeyed God's mandate to leave Ur, he simply gave up his past. But when he was summoned to Mount Moriah to deliver his own son to God, he was asked to surrender his future as well."[3]

Additionally, Genesis 22:3 reminds us of Abraham's deep love for this son. "Take your son, your only son, Isaac, whom you love," it reads. This was a good, an appropriate love, and no doubt an intimate and intense love from a father to his son and heir. The mere thought of plunging a knife into his chest must have been terrible for Abraham, much more so the act itself. Obedience required that Abraham know God and trust God with great confidence.

A GREAT PROBLEM FOR FAITH

Our passage, like Genesis 22, tells us that Abraham passed the test, that he obeyed God by faith. Verse 17 tells us, "By faith Abraham, when God tested him, offered Isaac as a sacrifice." The Genesis account is considerably more full:

> Early the next morning Abraham got up and saddled his donkey. He took with him two of his servants and his son Isaac. When he had cut enough wood for the burnt offering, he set out for the place God had told him about. On the third day Abraham looked up and saw the place in the distance. He said to his servants, "Stay here with the donkey while I and the boy go over there. We will worship and then we will come back to you."
>
> Abraham took the wood for the burnt offering and placed it on his son Isaac, and he himself carried the fire and the knife. . . . When they reached the place God had told him about, Abraham built an altar there and arranged the wood on it. He bound his son Isaac and laid him on

*the altar, on top of the wood. Then he reached out his hand
and took the knife to slay his son.* (Gen. 22:3–6, 9–10)

That remarkable account raises some questions for us.
How does faith overcome the natural objections to this command? How does faith pass this kind of test? I want to offer
four answers, beginning with this: faith kneels before God in
humble submission.

Abraham must surely have had a long night before setting
out with his son for the place of sacrifice. Surely he must have
reflected on the staggering demand God had made but also on
his right to make it. He must have thought about how much
he loved Isaac but also about his devotion to the Lord. While
unable to reason through all the problems, he must have
knelt before God, trusted him, and asked for grace to obey. It
is worth pointing out that this greatest test occurs at the end
of his life's journey of faith. His success here is the product of
earlier and lesser trials, many of which he failed, as God
honed and refined his character and his faith. Having received
this command, Abraham must have reckoned that God's will
is higher than his will. "Thy will and not mine be done," he
must have prayed, perhaps with tears at the thought of what
that required. Abraham's faith humbly knelt before God and
thus was able to obey God's command.

However much difficulty this test caused for Abraham,
the account of it has tried the faith of many more people.
Many people read these verses and recoil from the God who
speaks in them. How could a good God ask a father to kill a
son, they ask? Many people therefore reject the Bible on the
grounds of this supposedly twisted use of divine authority.
Moralists reject God, but existentialists reject Abraham, finding his faith impossible to embrace. The classic example is

Søren Kierkegaard, whose *Fear and Trembling* demanded to know how Abraham could be sure it was God speaking to him, how could a father do what Abraham went ahead and did? Surely this is not the kind of faith a decent, authentic existentialist wants to emulate!

How would Abraham respond to that? Surely he would have replied that he was a creature before the Creator. Abraham worshiped God as God and therefore did not think to place himself in the position of judge of the Most High and Lord of heaven. Abraham's faith was rooted in conscious humility; his faith knelt before the throne of a God he would no longer dare to judge.

Let me put this somewhat differently. Occasionally I will find myself talking with someone who is very disturbed about a subject like this test of Abraham's faith, or God hardening Pharaoh's heart in Exodus, or the Bible's teaching on the eternal bodily punishment of condemned sinners in hell. Inevitably, from the person's perspective, what God is doing is seen as a terrible thing. "How can a good God do something that is so wrong?" they are asking.

I always tell someone with that kind of difficulty that from the perspective of their humanism they are never going to receive an acceptable answer. By humanism, I mean that belief, so ingrained in us all, that what is best for the greatest number of humans is ultimately the yardstick of all good. Let me point out that God is not a humanist. God is a theist! God does not think that the greatest good for humans is the greatest good. He thinks that the glory of his name is paramount. He thinks that the manifestation of his justice and his holiness and, yes, his love are worth more than all the stars in the sky. He says, "Be still, and know that I am God; I will be exalted among the nations, I will be exalted in the earth" (Ps. 46:10).

When it comes to such disturbing matters as this command God gave to Abraham, our humanism will never be satisfied. God does not intend to satisfy our humanism but to drive us out from it. God is not going to satisfy our queries in judgment of him; God will not accept a position on the witness stand, while we presume to sit on the bench. It is only on our knees before a true God that we will receive and be able to accept satisfactory answers to questions like those regarding Abraham's test. Abraham was no longer a humanist; all his years exercising faith had taught him to humbly kneel before the Lord and put his trust in him.

In asking how Abraham resolved his problems and passed this test of faith, the second explanation is that the faith that receives God's promises must also obey God's commands. We see more than a hint of this in Hebrews. Who obeyed God's command? It was "he who had received the promises" (v. 17).

The point is that the same faith that receives and relies upon God's Word in the promise is obligated to receive and obey God's Word in the command. It is the same God and the same Word. This is what Job said to his wife, when she urged him to complain about what God had allowed to happen to him: "Shall we accept good from God, and not trouble?" (Job 2:10). Faith accepts promise and precept, commands and comforts, Christ as Lord as well as Christ as Savior, knowing that the one cannot be had without the other. Faith knows that the path of safety and of blessing is also the path of obedience. Pink writes, "Spiritual faith does not pick and choose: it fears God as well as loves Him."[4]

Yes, but you may object that in this case the promise and the command stand in stark opposition. The command can be obeyed only by undermining the promise. The answer to that objection is that the faith that obeys God's command leaves the means to God. If God has commanded it, then God knows what he is doing and is able to work it out for good. Indeed, this is one of the striking differences between the one who believes in God and the one who believes in self. Those who trust in God do not find their solace in being able to solve the puzzle, by adding up their mental arithmetic. Christians find peace when they know what God has revealed and commanded; even without understanding, faith accepts it as true because it comes from God.

In short, we believe that God knows better than we do. He, for one thing, has more and better information, even infinite data compared to our slim sample. God also has an infinitely higher capacity for processing and ordering that information. Furthermore, God does all this without sin, whereas Christians realize that sin has infected all the circuit boards of their mental computers. Thus believers are glad to trust God when he has spoken, having in his Word an infinitely better and surer guide than even our powers of reason.

The third explanation follows from this. Faith obeys even without answers, but we also must observe that faith gains understanding through God's Word. God tested not only Abraham's devotion but also his spiritual understanding. The reason he was able to succeed in this test was partly because of the answers he found in what God had already revealed.

This too our passage makes clear, telling us, "Abraham reasoned that God could raise the dead" (Heb. 11:19). This was not autonomous reason but faithful reasoning from what God had revealed. This explains Abraham's willingness to take his beloved son's life. He believed that God could raise him back to life from the dead. This statement in Hebrews is not found in Genesis, but it is proved there. Genesis 22:5

tells us that when Abraham arrived at the appointed place he said to his servants, "Stay here with the donkey while I and the boy go over there. We will worship and then we will come back to you." Notice what he said: "*We* will come back."

Where, then, did Abraham get the idea that if he killed his son God would raise him from the grave? First, he must have realized that God's promise required that Isaac be alive. If Isaac had to be alive and yet had to be killed, then God had to raise him from the dead. That makes sense, but surely there is something more. Remember all the circumstances of Isaac's conception and birth, when Sarah was far beyond childbearing age, all in a manner promised and predicted and produced by the power of God. All of this surely made clear to Abraham that God has power over life, and if over life then over death as well. That was the ultimate answer to Abraham's problem, as it is for all of ours; with the knowledge of God's power to take and give life, Abraham was able to obey.

Abraham's understanding came from faithful reflection on what God had earlier revealed about himself. Abraham did not have the Bible, none of which had yet been written, but he did have personal experience with God. We do have the Bible, and our faith will find power to obey by learning and understanding God's ways through the study of his Word.

Fourth and finally, and surely this is the most significant explanation, Abraham was able to obey because he knew and trusted God. Because he had really come to know God, to know what God is like, Abraham was able to trust him completely, to rely upon the Lord as his God, and to honor him by obeying. Philip E. Hughes explains:

> *Because he enjoyed a proper relationship with God Abraham knew that God is altogether holy and just and loving*

and that he cannot be untrue to himself; and he realized that it was not for him, a sinful, finite creature, to query the word of his infinite Creator. . . . This trial, in fact, so far from shaking Abraham's faith, actually served to estab-lish it, for through it the unchangeable character of God's purpose and the impossibility that God should prove false to his promise became more than ever the great motivating realities to him.[5]

That doesn't mean it wasn't hard for Abraham to obey. Abraham must have died a thousand times during the three days' march to the place where he would sacrifice the son he loved. But it does mean he was able to obey by faith. And it will mean that for you if you come to know God, to study and understand his attributes, to realize that because he is holy, then all his motives are holy, that because he is almighty nothing lies beyond his ability to save, that because he is good, as Paul wrote in Romans 8:28, "In all things God works for the good of those who love him." "Abraham reasoned that God could raise the dead," and a God like that was worthy of his trust.

THE PARABLE OF THE OFFERED SON

Verse 19 concludes our passage by saying, "And figura-tively speaking, he did receive Isaac back from death." That tells us how the story ended. As they walked up the mount, Isaac asked his father about the lamb for the burnt offering. "Where is the lamb?" he asked. To this, Abraham gave a great and provocative answer, "God himself will provide the lamb for the burnt offering, my son" (Gen. 22:8). That is faith and a real knowledge of God at work; it shows us how much Abraham was able to understand, although he lived at such a primitive time in redemptive history, because of his faith.

Genesis tells us how God provided for Abraham. As his knife began the arc that would end Isaac's life,

> the angel of the Lord called out to him from heaven, "Abraham! Abraham!" "Here I am," he replied. "Do not lay a hand on the boy," he said. "Do not do anything to him. Now I know that you fear God, because you have not withheld from me your son, your only son." Abraham looked up and there in a thicket he saw a ram caught by its horns. He went over and took the ram and sacrificed it as a burnt offering instead of his son. So Abraham called that place The LORD Will Provide. (Gen. 22:11–14)

You see why our passage in Hebrews therefore concludes, "And figuratively speaking, he did receive Isaac back from death." Isaac did not die and have to be resurrected, but God spared his life and honored Abraham's faith.

Christians have long seen the episode atop Moriah as a picture of God's provision of another sacrifice, the true sacrifice and Lamb of God. "Where is the lamb?" asked Isaac, just as the whole of the Old Testament asked that question. Years later in the Israelite priesthood, lamb after lamb was slain, day after day at the temple, yet all the while everyone knew they could not really take away their sin. "Where is the true lamb?" the priests and people must often have asked. The answer was finally given by the last prophet of the old dispensation, John the Baptist, who saw Jesus walking along the Jordan and cried out, "Look, the Lamb of God, who takes away the sin of the world!" (John 1:29).

It is interesting to note that the Greek text in Hebrews 11:19 does not say that Isaac's deliverance was "figuratively speaking" like a resurrection. The word it uses is *parable*, so that verse 19 literally reads, "Abraham reasoned that God could raise the dead, and as a parable, he did receive Isaac back from death." Christians have long understood this to mean that Isaac's death illustrated and pointed forward to another death, the true death that takes away our sin.

Indeed, the parallels are striking. Abraham was a father asked to sacrifice his son. We noted earlier that the expression "one and only son" doesn't exactly fit here, although Isaac was singular as the child of promise. But perhaps the real purpose of the phrase is to point us to another Father who did give his one and only Son as a sacrifice. John 3:16 tells us, "For God so loved the world that he gave his one and only Son, that whoever believes in him shall not perish but have eternal life."

There is considerably more to this. Isaac carried wood for the offering on his back, just as Jesus Christ would later carry his cross to his place of sacrifice. Abraham's and Isaac's journey through the valley of the shadow of death totaled three days, and for three days Jesus Christ lay in the tomb before he, as Isaac prefigures, was raised by the power of God. Clement of Alexandria, writing in the second century A.D., sees Isaac's deliverance as "an intimation of the divinity of the Lord . . . for Jesus rose again after his burial, having suffered no harm, like Isaac released from sacrifice."[6] Indeed, Christians have traditionally seen the ram in the thicket to symbolize Christ's human nature, offered up to death for us, and Isaac as Christ's divine nature, which though taken to the place of death is not allowed to die.

Those are interesting, indeed more than provocative parallels. But if we add them up, what does it mean for us? We considered earlier the repulsion people experience at the idea of a father being commanded to offer up his son to death. What, then, do we think of a Father who does this voluntarily, as God has done? If this repulses us it is only because we have forgotten or denied the essential fact of our situation, that we are sinners before a holy God. Indeed, I said earlier that only by bowing before God will we ever make sense of a passage like this, but now I must add that we can grasp it only by confessing the guilt of our sin and our need of a lamb to die like this for us. We must be the ones who cry out, "Where is the lamb? Where is the lamb for me?"

If we will cry that in faith, we will discover in God's Word the amazing fact that God the Father gave his one and only Son out of love for us. Romans 3:25 tells us, "God presented him as a sacrifice of atonement, through faith in his blood." Speaking of Jesus, Paul writes in Ephesians 1:7, "In him we have redemption through his blood, the forgiveness of sins, in accordance with the riches of God's grace." As Paul also says in Ephesians 1:6, all of this is "to the praise of his glorious grace, which he has freely given us in the One he loves."

We have seen that the key to accepting God's Word is to realize that God's glory, God's praise, is higher than human good. But here we find that in reality, for sinners, God's glory is also the source of our good, namely, our redemption in Christ's blood and the forgiveness of our sins. If that does not change our way of thinking about a Father offering up his Son, then I suppose nothing ever will. In the cross of Jesus Christ we find what Paul described as "how wide and long and high and deep is the love of Christ . . . [a] love that surpasses knowledge" (Eph. 3:18–19). That is the love that calls us to faith in God.

Therefore, whenever God tests our faith, tries our devotion to him, whenever God calls on us to say, "Your will be done," let us remember Jesus Christ, who faced his death on a cross for us with similar words. With blood-tinged drops of sweat upon his brow, Jesus prayed, "Father, if you are willing, take this cup from me; yet not my will, but yours be done" (Luke 22:42).

How great was Abraham's joy upon the mount. He named it for what had happened there, calling the place "The Lord Will Provide." We look back with greater joy to another mount, where another lamb was slain in our place, and we name it "The Lord Has Provided." Therefore, whenever God tests our faith, whenever he imposes his sovereign rights, it is a God who has purchased for us a free salvation, a full forgiveness, a costly redemption at the price of his Son's life. As Peter Lewis wrote:

> *The faith of Abraham may inspire us but it is the faith of Jesus that saves us, the Son who "humbled himself and became obedient unto death—even death on a cross" (Phil. 2:8). There is no atonement on Moriah but on Golgotha there is a once-for-all and perfect sacrifice for sin; it was what was done there that saves Abraham and Isaac and you and me.[7]*

It saves us, that is, if we turn to that Father and to his Son in faith, eager to receive what he has promised and willing to obey his Word, because we have come to know his love and trust his grace.

NINE

FAITH TRUSTING GOD'S PLAN

HEBREWS 11:20-22

*By faith Isaac blessed Jacob and Esau in regard
to their future. By faith Jacob, when he was dying, blessed each
of Joseph's sons, and worshiped as he leaned on the top of his
staff. By faith Joseph, when his end was near, spoke
about the exodus of the Israelites from Egypt and gave
instructions about his bones. (Heb. 11:20–22)*

When God came to Abraham, he entered into covenant not only with this one man but also with the generations that were to come through Abraham. "I will establish my covenant as an everlasting covenant between me and you and your descendants after you for the generations to come, to be your God and the God of your descendants after you" (Gen. 17:7). Therefore, when the record of Hebrews 11 moves past Abraham, we do not encounter random individuals but the generations that came from him. Verses 20–22 consider the faith of the heirs of the three generations that followed: Isaac, Jacob, and Joseph.

God not only made covenant with Abraham but also revealed much of his plan to him. This came about through promises and prophecies. God made great promises to Abraham that revealed something of his plan:

> As for me, this is my covenant with you: You will be the father of many nations. No longer will you be called Abram; your name will be Abraham, for I have made you a father of many nations. I will make you very fruitful; I will make nations of you, and kings will come from you. . . . The whole land of Canaan, where you are now an alien, I will give as an everlasting possession to you and your descendants after you; and I will be their God. (Gen. 17:4–6, 8)

In Genesis 15, God gave a particularly clear prophecy to Abraham: "The LORD said to him, 'Know for certain that your descendants will be strangers in a country not their own, and they will be enslaved and mistreated four hundred years. But I will punish the nation they serve as slaves, and afterward they will come out with great possessions. . . . In the fourth generation your descendants will come back here' " (Gen. 15:13–14, 16).

For the men we will study here those events were still future; they lived in the shadow of God's plan, revealed through promises and prophecy. Despite all their difficulties and weakness, they trusted God and responded in faith to the plan he had revealed. In Ephesians 1:11, the apostle Paul tells us that God has a plan, according to which he "works out everything in conformity with the purpose of his will." In Ephesians 3:10–11, Paul adds that this eternal purpose is accomplished in Jesus Christ and is for the praise of the glory and wisdom of God. In the midst of the dangers and uncertainties of their world, a world essentially like ours, Isaac, Jacob, and Joseph realized something of God's plan and put their trust in him.

THREE PORTRAITS OF RIPENED FAITH

Having given a great deal of attention to Abraham in verses 8–19, the writer of Hebrews quickly summarizes the faith of three patriarchs who followed: Isaac his son, Jacob his grandson, and Joseph his great-grandson. To summarize their faith, he looks at each of these three at the end of their lives, offering portraits of ripened faith that pick up on the statement made in verse 13: "All these people were still living by faith when they died."

First we view Isaac, the child of promise born to Abraham and Sarah, who, although he was the younger half-brother of Ishmael, received the covenant blessing. When Abraham died, the Lord came to Isaac to confirm the covenant with him: "To you and your descendants I will give all these lands and will confirm the oath I swore to your father Abraham. I will make your descendants as numerous as the stars in the sky and will give them all these lands, and through your offspring all nations on earth will be blessed" (Gen. 26:3–4). That is a recapitulation of the promise God had made to Abraham before him.

As we read the account of Isaac in the Book of Genesis, he does not come across as the boldest man of faith. His life was mostly uneventful while God blessed him richly. Most of the biblical material about him concerns the passing on of the blessing to his sons, Jacob and Esau. This is what the writer of Hebrews focuses on in verse 20: "By faith Isaac blessed Jacob and Esau in regard to their future."

Genesis 25 tells of the birth of these twin boys, Esau the older and Jacob the younger. They were born in answer to Isaac's and Rebekah's prayer for her barrenness. During her pregnancy the Lord informed Rebekah that the younger would receive the blessing (Gen 25:23), so they knew from the start this much of God's plan. Isaac, however, preferred Esau as the boys grew older; Genesis 25:28 tells us in unflattering terms that Isaac liked him better because Esau was a skillful hunter and Isaac "had a taste for wild game."

In one of the Bible's more famous episodes, Jacob tricked his aged and blind father into giving him the blessing instead of Esau. In this manner, the prophecy God had given was fulfilled and God's plan was upheld. Isaac had told Esau to kill some game and prepare his favorite dish, after which he would give him the blessing. But at his mother's urging, Jacob went to Isaac in his place, having covered himself with furs to present the feel and smell of Esau and bringing a meal like the one his father wanted. Isaac therefore gave Jacob the blessing he had intended for Jacob's twin.

Esau returned to find that Jacob had stolen the blessing, and he begged his father to undo what had happened. "Bless me—me too, my father!" Esau cried (Gen. 27:34). But Isaac, apparently recognizing the working of God's plan, knew he could not undo what had been done, and in giving such blessing as he had left, he informed Esau that he would serve his younger brother. Apparently the writer of Hebrews has in mind this response to God's providential control when he writes, "By faith Isaac blessed Jacob and Esau in regard to their future."

The Bible's account moves from Isaac to Jacob, and he too presents a less than sterling life history. What Jacob did to gain his father's blessing became a life pattern. He tricked his father to steal Esau's blessing, and he would go on to trick his father-in-law, Laban, of great flocks in order to make himself rich. Jacob's grasping tendencies did not truly bless him, for with each achievement he had to flee the anger of those he had wronged. Finally this pattern brought him to the end of his prodigious mental resources. Beside the Jabbok River, God wrestled Jacob into submission, and the grasper was made a man of faith (Gen. 32). God changed his name from Jacob to Israel, and thereafter he was a model believer. Hebrews 11:21 tells us about the end of his life, saying, "By faith Jacob, when he was dying, blessed each of Joseph's sons, and worshiped as he leaned on the top of his staff."

Jacob and his family had come to Egypt during a famine, where Joseph had become prime minister to the Pharaoh. Genesis 48 tells us of Jacob giving Joseph the blessing of the firstborn and then passing on his blessing to Joseph's two sons, Manasseh and Ephraim.

Hebrews 11:21 tells of two different episodes, the giving of the blessing and Jacob's request that Joseph promise to have him buried in the land of his fathers, a request we are told took place as he worshiped God while leaning on his staff. "Do not bury me in Egypt," he said, "but when I rest with my fathers, carry me out of Egypt and bury me where they are buried." "I will do as you say," Joseph answered. " 'Swear to me,' he said. Then Joseph swore to him, and Israel worshiped as he leaned on the top of his staff' " (Gen. 47:29–31).

This picture of Jacob worshiping God as he leaned on his staff, at the end of his strength, presents a beautiful picture of faith. It was fitting for Jacob to make this request in this way, for the staff was the sign of Jacob's pilgrimage. William L. Lane writes, "Jacob's final act of worship, leaning upon the top of his staff, was characteristic for one who lived his life as a stranger and a sojourner." We see why the writer of Hebrews chose this passage to summarize Jacob's life as a pilgrim believer, "who, in the face of death, lays claim to the future through the exercise of faith in the realization of the promises of God."[1]

Finally, we have Joseph, who by faith "when his end was near, spoke about the exodus of the Israelites from Egypt and gave instructions about his bones" (v. 22). Out of all the exciting events of Joseph's life this seems a strange summary, but it fits the approach of viewing their faith at the time of their death. Joseph's story is well known: betrayed by his brothers, he ended up a slave in Egypt. Trusting God, he was ultimately delivered and raised up to be prime minister to Pharaoh, with great power and wealth. When a famine struck Canaan, the family arrived as refugees only to find their long-lost brother as the keeper of Egypt's grain. Jacob, who had mistakenly thought Joseph dead, rejoiced, and the covenant family entered in for what would turn out to be a very long stay in Egypt.

Earlier we considered God's prophecy to Abraham, telling him of the events that now would transpire. His descendants would be aliens in another land, enslaved and mistreated for four hundred years, after which God would deliver them in a great exodus (Gen. 15:12–16). It is obvious that this prophecy stayed in the family, because Joseph knew of it and trusted what God had revealed about his plan. Therefore, as his death approached, he exhorted the others to believe the promise of deliverance and directed that his remains be taken out of Egypt when the exodus took place. Despite the fact that his wife and palaces and great riches were all in Egypt, even though his great achievements were there, the earthly monuments to his wisdom and skill in saving the nation from famine were there, Joseph knew that his future lay with the promises of God. To show this, and no doubt to encourage generations of Israel about the exodus to come, Joseph directed that his bones be taken for burial in the tomb of Abraham and Isaac and Jacob, in the promised land. If he could not live there in life, then he would go there in death, trusting in the God of the promise. John Calvin writes of him: "The fact that wealth, luxuries, and honours did not lead the holy man to forget the promise nor hold him back in Egypt, is a strong argument for faith."[2]

FAITH TRUSTING GOD'S PLAN

These three brief descriptions and the Genesis records to which they point exemplify everything we have seen in this chapter on faith. Hebrews 11:1 says, "Faith is being sure of what we hope for and certain of what we do not see." Surely that is what we find in the record of Isaac, Jacob, and Joseph, who trusted in things unseen, spiritual realities made tangible to them by faith. That is the first thing we want to say about their faith, that it was focused on spiritual realities. Their faith was rooted not in things of this world but in the things of heaven. In verses 9–10, the writer includes these patriarchs in the great statement about Abraham's faith: "By faith he made his home in the promised land like a stranger in a foreign country; he lived in tents, as did Isaac and Jacob, who were heirs with him of the same promise. For he was looking forward to the city with foundations, whose architect and builder is God."

These three family members had varied experiences, and each had his differences. But they all were looking to God for spiritual blessings while they lived like pilgrims in this world. In this way they showed that their citizenship was in heaven, and they each showed a mutual concern to pass on a spiritual inheritance to their children. We will diligently do the same if we possess a like faith.

The faith of these men was first spiritual, but second, it was forward-looking, as the passing of the blessing demonstrates. None of these men experienced the fulfillment of the promises when they died, but they were looking ahead to what God would do in the future. This is why they took the passing on of God's blessing so seriously. Isaac died knowing that God's plan would play out through his descendants, ultimately leading to his salvation. Joseph, especially, grounded his hope in a tangible understanding that although he was forced to live and serve in a foreign land, in the future God would provide a home for him, even in death.

Hebrews 11 emphasizes how faith handles the prospect of death, and this is a third feature of their faith. It is obvious that these men trusted in God's resurrection, for they faced death with a calm serenity, Jacob worshiping God while resting on his staff. It is always a mark of Christian faith to approach the reality of death with a peace that comes from God. Christian poetry and hymnody abound in expressions of trust in God in the face of death, of death as the entrance into life eternal, as in the lines of this Christian poem:

The pale horse stands and will not hide,
the night has come and I must ride;
But not alone to unknown lands,
My Friend goes with me holding hands.
I've fought the fight; I've run the race,
I now shall see him face to face,

Who called me to him long ago
and bade me trust and follow . . .
I'll mount and ride, no more to roam,
The pale horse bears me to my home.[3]

Fourth and finally, the faith of all three patriarchs was firmly fixed upon the word of God, and therefore upon the plan God revealed through it. They received God's revelation in faith, and in his plan they saw that they were joined to his great redemptive purpose, stretching back in history through Abraham and those before him and reaching forward toward eternity. They saw that they played a part in that plan, by God's grace, that they were links connecting others to God's true promised land. In the promises and prophecies of God's word they saw the substance of things to come just as we must, and they knew how to face the present as well as the future, which is what faith does for the believer.

GOD'S UNFAILING PLAN

If understanding God's plan was essential to these patriarchs, and if they are spoken of here in Hebrews 11 as models for our faith, then the plan of God must be of great importance to every Christian. Abraham and his descendants knew some things about what God had in store, and what they knew, what they had been told, they trusted. We have the whole Bible, which tells us far more, and what we have we too must trust.

The Bible shows that God's plan centers on the work of Jesus Christ for the salvation of sinners. It is in Christ that these promises to Abraham have come true. The apostle Paul, in Galatians 3:14–16, tells us that Jesus was the heir to whom these descendants pointed, the one in whom all God's promises are secured for us. Second Corinthians 1:20 says, "For no matter how many promises God has made, they are 'Yes' in Christ." Therefore, Paul says to believers, "Set your minds on things above, not on earthly things. For you died, and your life is now hidden with Christ in God" (Col. 3:2–3).

God's plan for history centered on the coming of Jesus Christ to bear the sin of the world and then to work a new principle into history through the faith of those who trust in him. That plan continues even now as the gospel is preached and lived out, as men and women come to faith, as parents pass it on to their children. It will continue until it culminates in the return of Christ in power, the judgment of all people, and the consummation of all things to the glory of God. That is what the plan of God is all about, and we are told of it plainly in the Scriptures.

But the Bible also makes plain that God has a plan for individual people. Paul spoke of this to the Athenians in Acts 17:26 and 28: "From one man [God] made every nation of men, that they should inhabit the whole earth; and he determined the times set for them and the exact places where they should live. . . . For in him we live and move and have our being." Perhaps the statement of God's plan that is best known to believers comes from Jeremiah 29:11, where God said to the generation in exile: " 'For I know the plans I have for you,' declares the LORD, 'plans to prosper you and not to harm you, plans to give you hope and a future.' "

Our passage in Hebrews 11 makes clear three things about God's plan, which Peter Lewis identifies in his study of these verses. First, we find here that God's plan cannot be manipulated. These patriarchs knew a great deal of information about their future, yet that did not give them control over events. Isaac illustrates this best. He wanted to give Esau the blessing, even though he knew God had foretold that it would go to Jacob. When he was old and blind, Isaac arranged to bless Esau, but the blessing was not Isaac's to give or to manipulate. Jacob's trickery in gaining the blessing may not commend his piety, but it does show God's ability to implement his plan.

One reason we cannot manipulate God's will is that we cannot discern it except as he has spoken in his Word. As Isaiah says, " 'For my thoughts are not your thoughts, neither are your ways my ways,' declares the LORD" (Isa. 55:8). Paul said in a doxology: "How unsearchable his judgments, and his paths beyond tracing out! Who has known the mind of the Lord? Or who has been his counselor?" (Rom. 11:33–34). Some people spend their time trying to figure out the details of God's plan, to decipher things such as the exact timing of Christ's second coming. But given the information of the Old Testament, we could not have even figured out his first coming! The Messiah was to be born in Bethlehem, he was to be called a Nazarene, and he was to come out of Egypt. Who could make sense of that in advance except the God who planned it?

If we know God has a plan but we cannot predict the future, what are we to do? We are to submit to God's Word. We are to trust and obey, step by step as God leads us through this world, like the pilgrims we are on our long journey home.

The second point Lewis makes from this passage is that God's plan cannot be taken for granted. Whenever we are sure of what God has in store for us, we are likely to be surprised. Joseph learned this lesson when he brought his two sons before Jacob to receive his blessing. Joseph carefully placed the older son, Manasseh, by Jacob's right hand, and Ephraim, the younger, by his left. The Bible describes what happened next: "But Israel reached out his right hand and put it on Ephraim's head, though he was the younger, and crossing his arms, he put his left hand on Manasseh's head, even though Manasseh was the firstborn" (Gen. 48:14). When Joseph saw his father's right hand on his younger son, Ephraim, he protested, "No, my father, this one is the firstborn, put your right hand on his head" (Gen. 48:18). But Jacob refused, and his crossed arms provide a firm reminder that we cannot assume God's plan or take it for granted.

This means we must expect to be surprised by God and that we must keep our eyes focused on him always. He will start things in unexpected places, do things through unexpected people, all to show that he is the one who is orchestrating this plan that works according to his secret will. How often it glorifies God to work in contrary ways, to work against normal expectations. He takes the chief of sinners and persecutor of the church, Saul of Tarsus, and makes him Paul, the great apostle of grace. He takes a sin-obsessed monk like Martin Luther and through him returns the gospel to the church. Today he makes Christianity burn brightest in poor, downtrodden places, in China and in the Third World. It glorifies him to work at cross-purposes to the wisdom of the world. He is "the God who gives life to the dead and calls things that are not as though they were" (Rom. 4:17).

Jacob's crossed arms remind us that God's plan is not subject to human standards and conventions. In the logic of the ancient world, the oldest son always received the chief blessing, but God operates differently. Indeed, none of the three figures in our passage were the oldest according to the flesh. Isaac, Jacob, and Joseph were all younger sons, but they were also the ones who received God's blessing. They received their position according to grace, by faith, and that is how God operates in the world. Therefore Philip E. Hughes rightly concludes, "The will of God cannot be forced into conformity with human patterns and preconceptions. His power manifests itself precisely within the sphere of human weakness. . . . The line of promise is not the line of the flesh but the line of faith."[4]

We all have plans. I have a plan for my life and God has a plan for my life, and I need to realize that his plan is different from mine! My plan is one that goes forward in a straight line, each work building on another, small successes leading to large ones. My plan calls for achievement and blessing and worldly comfort. But though I have a plan, I can be sure that God's is different. He takes my plan, edits it with sorrows and failures and weaknesses, and gives it back to me one trial at a time. Peter said in his first epistle: "Now for a little while you may have had to suffer grief in all kinds of trials. These have come so that your faith—of greater worth than gold, which perishes even though refined by fire—may be proved genuine and may result in praise, glory and honor when Jesus Christ is revealed" (1 Peter 1:6–7). We cannot know what God has in store, except that we will receive trials and tribulations, all of which are overcome by faith. We cannot take God's plan for granted, but him we may trust implicitly. We cannot know what tomorrow brings, but we know the God who brings it. This is why Jesus warned us not to take our plans too seriously:

> *Therefore I tell you, do not worry about your life, what you will eat or drink; or about your body, what you will wear. Is not life more important than food, and the body*

more important than clothes? . . . See how the lilies of the field grow. They do not labor or spin. Yet I tell you that not even Solomon in all his splendor was dressed like one of these. If that is how God clothes the grass of the field, which is here today and tomorrow is thrown into the fire, will he not much more clothe you, O you of little faith? . . . But seek first his kingdom and his righteousness, and all these things will be given to you as well. (Matt. 6:25, 28–30, 33)

God's plan cannot be manipulated, and we must not take it for granted. But, third, this passage shows us that God's plan cannot fail. Isaac was a weak man, Jacob was a cheat, and Joseph was a victim. Yet through these three generations, God steadily wove his plan toward the end he had designed. Into Egypt went his people, right on his schedule. Isaac sought to give the blessing to Esau, but God's plan overruled; Joseph lined up his sons before his father, only to watch Jacob cross his arms. Years later Pharaoh would determine to hold Israel in slavery, yet God's people would carry out Joseph's body in the exodus. Nothing can change or thwart God's will and plan. "I am God, and there is no other," he says. "I am God, and there is none like me. I make known the end from the beginning, from ancient times, what is still to come. I say: My purpose will stand, and I will do all that I please" (Isa. 46:9–10).

This means that we must not judge God's intentions by the appearance of our circumstances. God is working according to his plan, for the good of those who trust him. Lewis writes, "One thousand years with him is like a day. Like Joseph we can be sure of God's future and therefore of our future for these are one in Jesus Christ. That future may seem less substantial than the present but it will be real and glorious when the pyramids of Egypt are dust and the empires of men forgotten."[5]

Of one thing we may be perfectly sure, that Jesus Christ reigns now upon the throne of heaven and that history leads to his exaltation as Lord of lords. "Worthy is the Lamb, who was slain," sings the eternal choir, "to receive power and wealth and wisdom and strength and honor and glory and praise!" (Rev. 5:12). That is history's certain end, that "at the name of Jesus every knee should bow, in heaven and on earth and under the earth, and every tongue confess that Jesus Christ is Lord, to the glory of God the Father" (Phil. 2:10–11).

History has a revealed end in the exaltation of Christ. But history also has a central point, a fulcrum on which it turns, namely, that God's Son came and lived and died for us upon the cross. History is about him; it is "his story." Therefore, one thing is sure, God's plan leads us either to life through faith in Christ or death in condemnation for those who reject his name.

Finally, the certainty of God's plan tells us what we really need to know now, namely, that we are to serve him who is the Lord of that great plan. We are to put God's Word into practice in our lives, bearing testimony to Jesus Christ, who shows us God's plan fulfilled. "I am making everything new," he says (Rev. 21:5). "It is done. I am the Alpha and the Omega, the Beginning and the End. To him who is thirsty I will give to drink without cost from the spring of the water of life. He who overcomes will inherit all this, and I will be his God and he will be my son" (Rev. 21:6–7).

TEN

FAITH CHOOSING GOD

HEBREWS 11:23–26

*By faith Moses' parents hid him for three months
after he was born, because they saw he was no ordinary child,
and they were not afraid of the king's edict. By faith Moses,
when he had grown up, refused to be known as the son of
Pharaoh's daughter. He chose to be mistreated along with the
people of God rather than to enjoy the pleasures of sin
for a short time. He regarded disgrace for the sake of Christ as of
greater value than the treasures of Egypt, because he was
looking ahead to his reward. (Heb. 11:23–26)*

Undoubtedly the two most prominent figures of the Old Testament are Abraham and Moses. It is no surprise, then, that when the writer of Hebrews turns to the Old Testament for models of faith, he dwells longest on these two great men. Hebrews 11 tells us five things Abraham did by faith, and when it turns to the life of Moses, there are also five statements that begin, "by faith."

His account starts by telling us of his parents' faith and ends with the faith of the generation that followed Moses. Like all of us, his faith was the product of others' influence on him, and he made his mark in the faith of others he influenced for the Lord.

The faith of Moses was particularly useful for the author's purpose, since the grand design of the letter of Hebrews is to persuade Jewish Christians not to abandon Christ for Moses. Moses, he shows us, aligned himself with Christ, even in disgrace, and if they wanted to follow Moses' example, they would have to do so as Christians and not as Jews.

MOSES' CHOICE

Moses is commended here for a choice he made, and faith will always make itself known through its choices. "By faith Moses, when he had grown up, refused to be known as the son of Pharaoh's daughter. He chose to be mistreated along with the people of God rather than to enjoy the pleasures of sin for a short time" (Heb. 11:24–25). This passage seems to refer to an incident that, according to Stephen in Acts 7:23, took place when Moses was forty years old. Exodus 2:11–12 tells us that he took the side of the Israelites against the Egyptians, thus forfeiting his status as son of Pharaoh's daughter:

> One day, after Moses had grown up, he went out to where his own people were and watched them at their hard labor. He saw an Egyptian beating a Hebrew, one of his own people. Glancing this way and that and seeing no one, he killed the Egyptian and hid him in the sand.

Moses' story is well known. Although born of Hebrew slaves, he was reared the son of Pharaoh's daughter. Moses' parents had concealed him in a basket, which they let drift upon the Nile, trusting their baby to the Lord's care rather than let him be killed by Pharaoh's soldiers. Pharaoh, fearing the growing numbers of the Israelites, had decreed that all Hebrew baby boys be killed. As a result of God's providential working, Moses grew up with every advantage. Stephen's summary of his life tells us, "Moses was educated in all the wisdom of the Egyptians and was powerful in speech and action" (Acts 7:22).

As he came to maturity, it seems that Moses realized he had a choice before him, one that would determine his destiny. The choice was straightforward: would he identify himself with the Hebrew slaves or with the Egyptian masters? Faith demands that kind of choice, and it involves a yes and a no. People today want to make everything yes; if you say no you are narrow and negative. But Moses knew that a yes required a corresponding no. He said yes to his identity as an Israelite, as a son of Abraham and a follower of Yahweh, and deliberately said no to his status as a prince of Egypt, a son of Pharaoh's daughter and a servant to the gods of the Nile.

Let's consider all that Moses left by siding with the people of God. First, he left worldly honor and power behind. He "refused to be known as the son of Pharaoh's daughter." According to some traditions, Pharaoh had no sons, and Moses stood in line to ascend the throne. That is possible but not certain. What is certain is that he was aligned with the royal house in an age when royalty stood next to divinity. Phenomenal power and exaltation were his if he would retain his position in Pharaoh's house.

Second, he turned his back on the pleasures of sin, which are always available to such a high person, and which, it seems, were part and parcel of life in Pharaoh's court. Third, he turned his back on "the treasures of Egypt," which we know were very, very great.

That is an awful lot to give up. It must have been something very attractive that took Moses' eye off those things! Our passage tells us succinctly. Moses gave all that up for two things: first, for the privilege of mistreatment with the people of God, and second, to share in the disgrace of Christ. That is the choice Moses made. Charles Haddon Spurgeon says to him:

> O Moses, if you must needs join with Israel there is no present reward for you; you have nothing to gain but all to lose; you must do it out of pure principle, out of love to God, out of a full persuasion of the truth, for the tribes have no honors or wealth to bestow. You will receive affliction, and that is all. You will be called a fool, and people will think they have good reason for so doing.[1]

What an advertisement that is for Christianity! But it is a substantially true one. People will often try to evangelize others with promises of how wonderful it is to be a Christian. But Moses presents a truer picture. To be a Christian you must give up the world to embrace the cross. Once a teacher came to Jesus offering to follow wherever he went. Jesus replied, "Foxes have holes and birds of the air have nests, but the Son of Man has no place to lay his head" (Matt. 8:20). He exhorted his disciples to count the cost of following him, saying, "Any of you who does not give up everything he has cannot be my disciple" (Luke 14:33). Moses' choice is the choice all must make who would follow Jesus: the pleasures and treasures of Egypt or affliction with the people of God and fellowship in the cross of Christ.

But that present loss does not go uncompensated: it gains spiritual peace now and riches untold later. Moses' choice cost him honor with people but brought him honor with God and, as our passage shows, a name that shall be praised forever. As one scholar puts it, "Whatever Moses' social position if he had remained on as a member of Egyptian society all we would know of him now would be as a name on a mummy in the British Museum."[2] But instead we find his name recorded forever in the hall of God's beloved heroes.

MOSES' FAITH

What causes a man to make a choice like this? Our passage tells us quite frankly. It was "by faith" that Moses chose reproach over power, Israel over Egypt. When people encounter a choice like Moses', they often ascribe it to other motives, yet there are no other motives that credibly explain what he did.

We might, for instance, think that blood loyalty forced Moses' choice. But blood is not often this thick, to go from prince to slave. The Bible does not give this as Moses' motive. Well, then, it may have been a quirk in his character, an eccentricity that led him to choose so ridiculously. But everything points in the other direction: Moses was a man of distinction among the Egyptians, a man of respect among the rulers. Perhaps, then, it was a sudden excitement; perhaps he heard some fiery preacher and became idealistic for a time. But having forty years afterwards to consider what he did, Moses never repented, never regretted his choice. What, then, can account for a man making a choice like Moses did? The only answer is faith.

What was it that Moses believed? Mainly he believed the

Israelites, though slaves, were the people of God. He understood that the Egyptians, though wielding power and enjoying wealth, were in opposition to the true God, that their pleasures were sinful ones and Israel's afflictions were holy ones. Surely that means that he knew Israel's God, Yahweh, to be the true God, and the many gods of the Nile to be empty idols. If this were true, he knew it was better to be one of God's people, even in a state of affliction.

Where, we might ask, did such faith come from? Our passage tells us it came from his parents. Verse 23 summarizes their trust in the Lord: "By faith Moses' parents hid him for three months after he was born, because they saw he was no ordinary child, and they were not afraid of the king's edict."

Pharaoh had ordered the murder of Hebrew baby boys, so Moses' parents, Amram and Jochebed, hid him for three months after his birth, not fearing Pharaoh's decree. Verse 23 says they did this because they saw he was no ordinary child. The Greek text says they saw that he was beautiful. In some way, they looked at Moses and saw that he was special, and thus they determined to risk themselves to save his life. Amram and Jochebed were motivated by something more than normal paternal love, by faith that the Lord had given them a special child.

According to the Jewish historian Josephus, Amram had received a dream in which he was told that this child would deliver Israel. If that story is true, it is consistent with what the Old Testament shows of other notable births, such as that of Jacob, and later of Samson and Samuel, and ultimately of Jesus Christ. At the least, Moses' parents saw in the striking beauty of their son a sign of divine grace that motivated them to take their stand. Verse 23 says that by faith they guarded him, and it was surely by faith that they later sent their newborn into the Nile, where he was discovered by Pharaoh's daughter.

One detail lends credence to the idea that Moses' parents knew he was born to be a deliverer and that they later told this to him. In Acts 7:25, Stephen speaks of Moses' murder of the Egyptian and says: "Moses thought that his own people would realize that God was using him to rescue them." Moses' knowledge of this calling as deliverer, therefore, at least partly motivated his choice to take a stand with Israel.

Moses got his faith the old-fashioned way, from his parents. He got it from what they taught him about the Lord and his covenant with Israel and his promises of a land and a multitude of seed. He got it, most especially, from their example of faith. The very thing that verse 27 commends Moses for, that he did not fear the king's anger, is first ascribed to his parents. This is how we pass on the faith to our children: by our words, but more pointedly by our actions. Children are either hardened by the hypocrisy of their parents, or like Moses they are inspired by their consistency between word and deed.

Surely Moses' experience as a prince providentially aided his budding faith. One of the great problems of state in that day was the problem of the Hebrew slaves. That was why Pharaoh tried to kill Moses and his generation of babies, because in keeping with God's promise to Abraham they were increasing like the sands on the seashore. The Book of Exodus begins with this dilemma that confronted the Egyptians, as described by Pharaoh:

> "Look," he said to his people, "the Israelites have become much too numerous for us. Come, we must deal shrewdly with them or they will become even more numerous and, if

war breaks out, will join our enemies, fight against us and leave the country." (Exod. 1:9–10)

How many times must Moses have heard of this problem in the schools and palaces of Pharaoh. He may have attended seminars on "the Israelite problem," with tips on how to oppress and afflict them, all caveated with the fact that nothing seemed to keep them down. Moses must have thought about the things his parents taught him, that the true God was with the people of Israel, that he had promised them great increase, and what is more, that God had promised them a home in a land of promise. This, too, is how parents pass on faith to their children, by teaching them to think biblically about the world and their times.

Because of his parents' faith, Moses grew up conscious of his identity and believing the promises of the Lord to the afflicted people of Israel. They gave to Moses that which any child needs most: faith in the Lord. It was "by faith" that Moses chose and identified with the people of God.

FAITH'S CALCULATION

We have seen a number of examples in these studies in Hebrews 11 of the relationship between faith and works. Faith always works, as we saw earlier in the example of Noah. Noah's belief that the flood was coming caused his axe to chop down trees and his hammer to build the ark. Abraham believed God's promise, and so he offered Isaac as God commanded. Moses, too, had faith, and his faith reckoned, his faith made calculations, and those calculations led to his actions.

That is what this passage says about Moses' faith, that his

choice was the result of faith's calculation. Verse 24 says, "he chose," and verse 25 tells us why, namely, "he regarded." According to faith's calculation, Moses "regarded disgrace for the sake of Christ as of greater value than the treasures of Egypt, because he was looking ahead to his reward." Moses provides yet another example of the principle of Hebrews 11:6, that faith believes God rewards those who earnestly seek after him. Moses wanted what was best, as we all do, and according to the calculation of faith he chose present affliction over pleasure, the disgrace of Christ over the treasures of Egypt. He put these side by side, and by faith he reckoned contrary to sight, considering the one as greater than the other.

Moses looked upon the honor of being Pharaoh's daughter's son, and by faith he saw that this distinction meant apostasy from God. Adoption in the ancient world normally severed ties to the old familial relationship. To be Pharaoh's relative, even if it meant gaining the throne and crown of Egypt, meant losing his status as an Israelite and therefore losing the covenant with God. So by faith, Moses reckoned that he was choosing between Pharaoh, a king, and Yahweh, the one true God. Based on that calculation he made his choice.

Likewise, he looked on the carnal pleasures of Pharaoh's court. J. C. Ryle comments: "Faith told Moses that worldly pleasures were 'pleasures of sin'. They were mingled with sin, they led on to sin, they were ruinous to the soul, and displeasing to God. It would be small comfort to have pleasure while God was against him. Better suffer and obey God, than be at ease and sin."[3] Reckoning that way, he willingly gave them up. The same is true of the vast treasures that would be his as an Egyptian prince. They were worldly treasures, temporary treasures, of no account compared with the spiritual and eternal riches that come through faith in God.

How many will look upon Moses' choice and cry, "What a fool! To have all that—honor, power, pleasure, wealth—and throw it away! These are the very things vast multitudes spend their lives seeking to gain only a portion of! And here Moses throws it all away! What folly! What a tragedy!" What would Moses say to that? I think he would say two words, from verse 26 in our text: "of Egypt." What treasures did he cast away? They were treasures that he knew, treasures of Egypt, which he then compared with the riches of God. To that Moses would have added four more words, from verse 25: "for a short time." The pleasures of sin he rejected were "for a short time." Or, as Spurgeon puts it, they were "for a season." He speaks for Moses when he hears a bell ringing in the air behind those words, saying:

> Did you hear the tolling of a bell? It was a knell. It spoke of a new-made grave. This is the knell of earthly joy—"For a season!" Honoured for doing wrong—"For a season!" Merry in evil company—"For a season!" Prosperous through a compromise—"For a season!" What after that season? Death and judgment.[4]

This is how Moses' faith made its calculation, and once we accept his principle, we do not marvel at his choice. What did faith tell him but that a reward awaited him in heaven that far outweighed any treasures of the Nile? As Paul would later reckon, "I consider that our present sufferings are not worth comparing with the glory that will be revealed in us" (Rom. 8:18). Faith showed Moses a crown that does not fade, a glory that shines with heaven's light. And faith showed

Moses how to reckon the afflictions of God's people. Ryle puts it this way:

> *Faith told Moses that affliction and suffering were not real evils. They were the school of God, in which He trains the children of grace for glory; the medicines which are needful to purify our corrupt wills; the furnace which must burn away our dross; the knife which must cut the ties that bind us to the world. . . .*
>
> *Marvel not that he refused greatness, riches and pleasure. He looked far forward. He saw with the eye of faith kingdoms crumbling into dust, riches making to themselves wings and fleeing away, pleasures leading on to death and judgment, and Christ only and His little flock enduring for ever. . . . He saw with the eye of faith affliction lasting but for a moment, reproach rolled away, and ending in everlasting honour, and the despised people of God reigning as kings with Christ in glory.*[5]

That is what faith showed Moses as he looked upon the kingdoms of this world, upon the pleasures and treasures of the Nile. I wonder what your faith sees as you look around you? Do you see things here that you must have? Do you see things now that you must enjoy? Do you see the affliction of God's people and turn away, the reproach of Christ of which you want no part? Then you see with different eyes, a different faith than Moses did, and you shall have a different reward.

Moses might have thought differently, and few would have complained. He might have thought that to spurn the love of his adopted mother was surely an evil thing. But instead he knew that God is greater than any mother or father or lover or friend; when there was a choice to be made he must choose for God. Or he might have listened to the thought that by remaining an Egyptian, by suppressing his convictions, by concealing his allegiance, he could do more good than he could by leaving. He might have been like those who stay where they have no business belonging, like Lot sitting in Sodom's gate. This is the myth of influence that afflicts so many out-of-place believers today. "It is true that I am allied with unbelief, with injustice, with evil," they say, "but it is worth the good that I can do." Moses did not rationalize this way. He might have thought of the example of Joseph before him, who stayed in Pharaoh's court, though Joseph was able to do so without participating in sin or committing apostasy. But Moses knew his situation was different, his times were different, and his conscience cried against the thought of association with evil.

Sometimes believers are called to serve in worldly courts. Obadiah rescued the prophets as chamberlain to Ahab, but he served there in great fear and at the daily risk of his life. Daniel served the king of Babylon, not in honor and wealth and pleasures of sin but in the den of lions and with his heart daily turned toward Jerusalem. Yes, some few are called to serve and aid the pharaohs of this world, but they are few and far between, and let their conscience be clean as to their calling, let them serve there out of a desire to honor God and not to deny him. Moses knew his heart, he knew his times, and his faith led him to obedience and not some worldly scheme of influence.

Moses might have sought a compromise to avoid so costly a choice, such an unpleasant decision and costly separation. He might have been Moses the Israelite in the court of Pharaoh. But surely he knew that if the Lord is God, he must serve him and not the gods of Egypt. If the Hebrews were his people, then he must not wear Egyptian colors. If affliction as a slave was his calling, he must not seek pleasure and honor. How much this way of thinking cuts across the grain of our relativistic age, our age of tolerance, our age of easy belief, of yes and no together. But to Moses' everlasting credit, for him there was no half-hearted allegiance, no faint commitment, no looking back upon the city of sinful pleasure. He knew what James would say in his epistle, that God will not reward the double-minded man (James 1:8). By faith Moses "chose to be mistreated along with the people of God rather than to enjoy the pleasures of sin for a short time. He regarded disgrace for the sake of Christ as of greater value than the treasures of Egypt, because he was looking ahead to his reward."

"WITH CHRIST"

I want to conclude by considering the remarkable statement that Moses was disgraced "for the sake of Christ." In what sense can we say that Moses believed on Jesus who came so many centuries later? That is surely an important point for the writer of Hebrews, since it was his design to motivate his Jewish Christian readers to follow Moses' example of suffering for the name of Christ.

There are a couple of ways we might think of Moses looking to Christ. The first recognizes the parallel in this passage between the people of God and Christ. In our passage, mistreatment with God's people is seen as essentially the same as disgrace for Christ's sake. Perhaps the writer of Hebrews had in mind Psalm 89:50–51 (NASB), which says, "Remember, O Lord, the reproach of Your servants . . . with which Your enemies have reproached, O LORD, with which they have reproached the footsteps of Your anointed." *Christ* means "Anointed," and here it is applied not to Jesus specifically but to the people of God.

Moses did not choose affliction as such, but rather affliction with the people of God. And what a difference those few words make, the difference between sorrow and joy, between loss and the greatest of gain. Spurgeon writes, " 'Affliction' nobody would choose; but 'affliction with the people of God,' ah! that is another business altogether. . . . Affliction with the people of God is affliction in glorious company. . . . 'With the people of God': that is the sweet which kills the bitter of affliction."[6]

"With the people of God" is where you always want to be, because that is where God is working with a purpose for good. There true wonders are seen, saving grace is found, flowers bloom in the desert, and a river flows that makes glad the city of God, in blessing or in affliction. To the mind of faith, with the people of God is always the place to be; it is where we belong, and where we will be so far as we are able to choose. If need be we will be with the people of God as slaves in Egypt, so that we might also be with them as God's royal children in glory forever.

That is one way of looking at Moses' sharing in disgrace, but for the writer of Hebrews the Christ unquestionably means the Lord Jesus Christ. His point is that Moses' faith was faith in Jesus. The Gospels plainly state this fact. When Nathanael brought his brother Philip to meet Jesus, he did so with these words: "We have found the one Moses wrote about in the Law . . . Jesus of Nazareth, the son of Joseph" (John 1:45). In John 5:46, Jesus said to the Jews, "If you believed Moses, you would believe me, for he wrote about me." On the Mount of Transfiguration, who was standing with

Christ and with Elijah, appearing in glory and speaking about the cross to come, but Moses (Luke 9:30). Surely much, even most, of what Moses came to know about Jesus came after this episode in his life, after this decision to leave the house of Pharaoh. But this much he surely knew: he knew that God would send a Savior to bring a kingdom; he knew that before the crown there lay a cross.

Moses' disgrace was one with that of Christ. It fit the pattern that Christ would later perfect in obedience and suffering. "He knew that the prizes of earth were contemptible compared with the ultimate reward of God"7—and that is the way of Christ, that is the way of fellowship in his sufferings. "Blessed are you," Jesus said, "when people insult you, persecute you and falsely say all kinds of evil against you because of me. Rejoice and be glad, because great is your reward in heaven" (Matt. 5:11–12). That is the choice Moses made; that is the reward he sought. And thus he could say along with Paul in Philippians 3:8, "I consider everything a loss compared to the surpassing greatness of knowing Christ Jesus my Lord, for whose sake I have lost all things. I consider them rubbish, that I may gain Christ."

Each of us must make that choice, and faith will make it wisely. Jesus said, "Whoever acknowledges me before men, I will also acknowledge him before my Father in heaven" (Matt. 10:32). Acknowledging Christ is always costly; it means yes not just to him but also to the affliction of his people, to his disgrace before the world. And it demands a no as well, for Jesus also said: "Anyone who does not take his cross and follow me is not worthy of me. Whoever finds his life will lose it, and whoever loses his life for my sake will find it" (Mt. 10:38–39).

ELEVEN

FAITH PASSING THROUGH

HEBREWS 11:27–29

By faith he left Egypt, not fearing the king's anger;
he persevered because he saw him who is invisible. By faith he
kept the Passover and the sprinkling of blood, so that the
destroyer of the firstborn would not touch the firstborn of Israel.
By faith the people passed through the Red Sea as on
dry land; but when the Egyptians tried to do so,
they were drowned. (Heb. 11:27–29)

In the Book of Hebrews the writer has appealed to a number of Old Testament examples, some of which are positive, as we have seen in this eleventh chapter, while others are negative. Chief among the negative examples is that of the generation that left Egypt in the exodus. The writer of Hebrews dwelt upon them in chapters 3 and 4, repeatedly referring to their complaints and rebellions. His main text was Psalm 95, which warned later generations of Israel against such unbelief: "Today, if you hear his voice, do not harden your hearts as you did in the rebellion, during the time of testing in the desert" (Heb. 3:7–8; Ps. 95:7–11).

The exodus is the great event of the Old Testament, and in the New Testament it is the dominant paradigm for Christian salvation. Now, in our passage from Hebrews 11, the author's record of faith brings us to this time, to Moses and the generation he led out of Egypt. Despite their many failures and rebellions and subsequent judgment from God, that generation did perform one great act of faith, the exodus and the subsequent passage through the Red Sea.

These verses, however, focus on Moses, the leader of God's people in the exodus. We find here that faith makes godly leadership courageous and that such leadership is able to reproduce its faith in the lives of others.

FROM FEAR TO FAITH

This passage begins by presenting us with an exegetical problem, dealing with Moses leaving Egypt. Verse 27 says, "By faith he left Egypt, not fearing the king's anger; he persevered because he saw him who is invisible." The question is this: To which one of Moses' departures does this refer? Is it his first departure, told to us in Exodus 2:15, after he had killed the Egyptian overseer, or is it the much later departure in the exodus?

An initial reading suggests the earlier departure, since this keeps the verses in historical sequence. The chief problem with this interpretation, however, is that it seems to contradict the Old Testament record. Exodus 2:14 explicitly says Moses was afraid, and verse 15 shows him fleeing from Pharaoh. Our passage says he did not fear the king's anger when he fled, and for this reason many commentators insist this must refer to the later occasion. Among these are John Calvin, John Owen, and B. F. Westcott. According to their view, this must refer to the time of the exodus, when Moses so courageously stood before Pharaoh and sent the plagues from God.

This assessment, however, presents two main problems. First, verse 27 thus refers to the exodus, which then is followed by the keeping of the Passover, although the latter happened first. The writer of Hebrews has been following a straightforward historical progression, which now would be broken. A possible answer is that verse 27 gives a summary that the next two verses then fill out.

The second problem is, I think, far more serious. Why did the writer of Hebrews go out of his way to make this point? There is no reason to mention Moses' lack of fear in reference to the exodus, since Pharaoh and the Egyptians were pleading for the Israelites to leave. But if this incident refers to the earlier departure, we see well why the writer of Hebrews mentions it. Given the importance of Moses' faith to the overall argument of this letter, he would seek to explain the statement about Moses' fear in Exodus 2:14. Yes, Exodus says Moses was afraid, but, the writer clarifies, we should not think it was fear of Pharaoh; his leaving then was by faith, since he knew that God had called him to deliver the people. Moses' abortive attempt to free the people failed and, yes, Moses became afraid, but his faith in God overcame his fear, and he left to await God's timing.

Following this reasoning, I think it more likely that verse 27 refers to the earlier departure, when Moses was forty years old, therefore serving as a fitting conclusion to what verses 25 and 26 said. Five statements in this record of Moses begin with the words "by faith," and together they chronicle his life and ministry. By faith his parents hid him, by faith he chose God's people over Pharaoh's house, by faith he left Egypt for Midian, by faith he kept the Passover (which sums up the whole period of his return as deliverer), and by faith he led the people through the Red Sea waters.

That interpretation of verse 27 cannot be certain, but we can be sure of the writer's point in this verse. We remember that this letter was written to Jewish Christians undergoing persecution, or at least the threat of it. If, as I think most likely, the setting was Rome and persecution from Caesar could be avoided by renouncing Christ and returning to Judaism, then quite a parallel existed between Moses' experience and theirs. The writer of Hebrews is therefore using this example to make the point that fear must be met with faith. This is a strong theme in the account about Moses. We are told his parents hid him because "they were not afraid of the king's edict" (v. 23). Now Moses left Egypt, not fearing the king's anger but seeing "him who is invisible." Likewise these Christians must not shrink back in the hour of their trial. In the face of Caesar's persecution, a king not unlike Pharaoh, they must stand firm in their faith in God.

How did Moses stand firm, and how could they expect to do the same? The answer is given at the end of this verse: "he persevered because he saw him who is invisible."

This is always how God's people triumph over threatening circumstances. It was how David beat Goliath. The giant mocked young David, but he replied, "You come against me with sword and spear and javelin, but I come against you in the name of the LORD Almighty" (1 Sam. 17:45). This was how Daniel's three friends stood firm before the king of Babylon, even to the point of being cast into the blazing furnace.

They saw their Lord, invisible to sight but evident to faith. When the king saw them untouched amid the flames he cried out, amazed that a fourth figure who looked like God was with them (Dan. 3:25). That was how Moses faced his early failure, his need to flee rather than fight, and his long decades of waiting for God's timing as he lived in the desert. The great New Testament statement of this principle is given by Paul in 2 Corinthians 5:7, "We live by faith, not by sight."

A great Christian example comes from the Scottish Reformer John Knox. Asked how he could so boldly confront the Roman Catholic queen, Knox replied, "One does not fear the Queen of Scotland when he has been on his knees before the King of Kings." It is said that the great conqueror Napoleon would sometimes call his generals in one by one before a great battle, to gaze on them without speaking and let them look upon his face. In a similar way, the man or woman of frequent communion with God will see his face in the midst of the fight, thereby finding courage and a strong incentive to faith.

FAITH KEEPING GOD'S WORD

The statement that Moses "saw him who is invisible" may be pointing to the burning bush, an awesome and pivotal event when Moses saw God. The emphasis, however, seems to be on a continuing spiritual perception. This is fully in keeping with the point of this chapter, that faith is being "certain of what we do not see" (Heb. 11:1). Moses was sure of God's promise and certain therefore of the future. He left Egypt awaiting God's timing for that future to be made real.

Undoubtedly the years of waiting were longer than Moses thought possible, forty years in all, as Acts 7:23 tells us. Initially the change might have been refreshing, but ten years and advancing age would have tried Moses' faith. As the ten turned to twenty, and then thirty, and finally forty, his confidence must have drained away, his sense of calling vanished into a dim if not bitter memory. Yet God was working with a purpose in his life, until the time had come for Moses to go back. Peter Lewis comments:

> Moses had to learn to be a servant not a master, a prophet not a prince, the friend of God not of Pharaoh. And so God stripped him of his advantages and began his apprenticeship in spiritual leadership. . . . Moses spent his first forty years becoming a somebody, then his second forty years becoming a nobody and then God could use him. . . . It was an apprenticeship in faith.[1]

Moses, no doubt impressed by the burning bush and the dramatic calling to return as Israel's deliverer, went back knowing that his leadership must be marked by faith, for it was faith that gave him endurance for those long and difficult years. Exodus 4–10 shows his bold confrontations with Egypt's king, in which he delivered one plague after another against unbelieving Pharaoh. Hebrews 11:28 points to the end of this drama, the tenth and final plague on the firstborn. God had said to Moses: "I will bring one more plague on Pharaoh and on Egypt. After that, he will let you go from here. . . . About midnight I will go throughout Egypt. Every firstborn son in Egypt will die, from the firstborn son of Pharaoh, who sits on the throne, to the firstborn son of the slave girl, who is at her hand mill, and all the firstborn of the cattle as well" (Exod. 11:1, 4–5).

Thus was celebrated the first Passover, which verse 28

describes as an incident of great faith by Moses. God told Moses the Israelites were to sacrifice a lamb without defect and to spread its blood on the doorframe of their houses. The angel of death, seeing the blood, would pass over, and the terrible plague would not visit them (Exod. 12:1–13). Under Moses' direction Israel did this and thus was spared, while loud laments filled the homes of Egypt.

We see Moses' faith at work here in a number of ways. First, the various plagues pitted the visible gods of Egypt against the invisible God who stood behind Moses. One after one, the Egyptian idols were disgraced in the plagues: Hapi, god of the Nile; Hekht the frog; Amen Ra the sun god. Each of these among others was mocked by the various plagues God sent: the plague of blood in the river, the plague of frogs, the plague of darkness, and so on. Moses feared not a god fashioned out of visible materials but the unseen and true God. Moses believed the word of the Lord, and he and his people were saved. But Pharaoh hardened his heart, and by his unbelief he and his people were broken.

Thus came the first Passover. It is unclear how much Moses perceived about its significance. God told him that the blood of the lamb would cause the destroyer angel to pass over, and probably without fully understanding he nonetheless acted out of faith. This seems to be the main point of the verse, that Moses by faith acted in careful observance of what God had said. Therefore, when we put verses 27 and 28 together, we see a clear contrast. Faith does not fear or listen to the world, to its powers and rulers, but faith does fear and does listen to God, carefully obeying all his Word. Moses kept God's word just as he was told, and in that manner he and countless others were saved from the wrath of God. The same holds true for everyone who hears God's Word and believes.

THE PASSOVER LAMB

There is another way in which verse 28 speaks of great faith, and it has to do with the blood of the lamb. We can imagine the thoughts of the Egyptians when the Israelites brought the lambs into their homes, then killed them and spread the blood around their doorposts. They were familiar with animal sacrifices, but as the Book of Hebrews has pointed out (Heb. 10:1–4), they must have realized that the blood of a helpless animal gave no protection, no real help against what was coming. Through the eyes of faith Israel saw another, greater sacrifice, one that is necessary because of our sin and that protects us forever from the holy wrath of God.

Regardless of how well Moses' generation understood the full meaning of the Passover lamb, the connection would have been clear to the original Christian readers of this letter. They would recognize the point that they must be saved the same way as Moses. God's wrath would come upon the city of man, and it would certainly fall on their godless oppressors. But if they wanted to escape the death such judgment brings, being themselves sinners, they like Moses must be found secure behind the blood of Jesus Christ. Philip E. Hughes explains the connection:

> As the Passover lamb was required to be perfect and unblemished and its sacrifice was the moment of the people's moving from bondage to liberty, so Christ is the fulfillment of all that was symbolized by this event: he is "the Lamb of God" (Jn. 1:29, 36), "our paschal lamb" (1 Cor. 5:7), whose precious redeeming blood is "like that of a lamb without blemish or spot" (1 Pet. 1:19), and who

through his death has destroyed the power of the devil, our spiritual Pharaoh, and delivered us from lifelong bondage (Heb. 2:14).[2]

Thus faith's most important act is to lay hold of Christ as Lamb of God, to trust him to remove our sin and preserve us against the coming of God's sure and holy wrath. Hughes quotes John Chrysostom, who long ago said:

If the blood of a lamb then preserved the Jews unhurt in the midst of the Egyptians and in the presence of so great a destruction, much more will the blood of Christ save us, for whom it has been sprinkled not on our doorposts but on our souls. For even now the destroyer is still moving around in the depth of night; but let us be armed with Christ's sacrifice, since God has brought us out from Egypt, from darkness and from idolatry.[3]

It was this that Moses laid hold of by faith in the Passover lamb's blood. Therefore, if these Jewish Christians were to fall back on to Moses from Christ, from the new covenant back to the old, they would be abandoning that by which Moses was saved, his faith in Christ's work for salvation.

FAITH PASSING THROUGH

Verse 29 concludes the account of Moses and his generation by speaking of their departure from the land of Egypt: "By faith the people passed through the Red Sea as on dry land; but when the Egyptians tried to do so, they were drowned."

This account from Exodus 14 is well known. After the

plague of the firstborn, Pharaoh and all the Egyptians had insisted on the Israelite's departure, even supplying them with great riches for the journey. Yet, Pharaoh's heart was hardened once again and he chased after them with his chariots. The Israelites were horrified, and cried out against Moses that God was allowing their destruction. Then, in Exodus 14:13–14, Moses gave his great reply, one that resounds all through the Bible:

> Do not be afraid. Stand firm and you will see the deliverance the LORD will bring you today. The Egyptians you see today you will never see again. The LORD will fight for you; you need only to be still.

Given the fact that the Egyptians were bearing down from the rear and that ahead of them lay the impassable Red Sea, that was quite a statement of faith. But Moses had learned that God's promise to deliver was certain of success. By faith he exhorted the people, and God rewarded Moses with this response:

> Raise your staff and stretch out your hand over the sea to divide the water so that the Israelites can go through the sea on dry ground. I will harden the hearts of the Egyptians so that they will go in after them. And I will gain glory through Pharaoh and all his army, through his chariots and his horsemen. The Egyptians will know that I am the LORD when I gain glory through Pharaoh, his chariots and his horsemen. (Exod. 14:16–18)

Here was the point of no return, and although the people needed prodding, they stepped forward into the divided sea.

Like many other believers, they saw no way of escape until God revealed it to the eyes of their faith.

This provides one of the great pictures of God's salvation, a salvation by grace alone that nonetheless requires us to step forward in saving faith. This is the only way anyone ever is saved, that God makes a way amid the raging fury of his wrath. It points us to Jesus Christ, who said, "I am the way, and the truth, and the life" (John 14:6). Just as Moses' staff parted the waves, so Christ Jesus was lifted up "that everyone who believes in him may have eternal life" (John 3:14).

John of Damascus, writing in the eighth century A.D., used this example of God's saving grace as an incentive to Christian praise:

> Come, ye faithful, raise the strain
>   of triumphant gladness;
> God hath brought his Israel
>   into joy from sadness;
> Loosed from Pharaoh's bitter yoke
>   Jacob's sons and daughters;
> Led them with unmoistened foot
>   through the Red Sea waters.

Moses understood this as a singular and epochal deliverance. His song to the Lord celebrates a sovereign grace and mighty salvation:

> I will sing to the LORD,
>   for he is highly exalted.
> The horse and its rider
>   he has hurled into the sea.
> The LORD is my strength and my song;

he has become my salvation. . . .
  The LORD *will reign*
    for ever and ever. (Exod. 15:1–2, 18)

That is the right conclusion, to praise God and to rest our faith on his saving power that will protect us from every foe.

SALVATION BY FAITH

Let me conclude with three observations, the first of which deals with Moses as a leader. The key aspect of Moses' leadership, as with all Christian leadership, was his faith. What, after all, do Christian leaders seek, but to inspire and instill faith in others? Moses' success as a godly leader consisted not only in his salvation but also in passing on his faith to others.

Moses shows us the value of leadership that inspires faith. He was the recipient of that kind of inspiration. We saw this in Joseph, who ordered that his bones be taken up out of Egypt with the exodus, as an intentional reminder to his descendants of God's promise of deliverance. Moses remembered that promise, because when he left he took Joseph's bones, and the patriarch's faith must have made a strong impression on him. Moses' parents also set a strong example of faith, and their impact was felt through the faith of their son, who led so many others out to their salvation. His example is an excellent reminder to every Christian leader along the lines of what Paul later wrote to Timothy: "Watch your life and doctrine closely. Persevere in them, because if you do, you will save both yourself and your hearers" (1 Tim. 4:16).

The second observation concerns what I consider the main point of this passage, the call to faith as the antidote to fear and danger. We have already noted that this passage corresponds powerfully to the original readers' situation as they met with persecution. Moses, like his parents, set an example of fearless courage in the face of worldly power. But the greatest encouragement comes in verse 28, where we see God intervening for the sake of his people. John Owen rightly comments on the death of the Egyptians in the Red Sea:

> When the oppressors of the church are closest to their own ruin they often rage most and are most obstinate in their bloody persecutions. It is the same to this day among the anti-Christian enemies of the church. . . . The destruction of the Egyptians, with Israel's deliverance being secured, was a type and pledge of the victory that the church will have over its anti-Christian adversaries.[4]

Third and finally, this passage makes plain the difference between faith and unbelief. Unbelief fears the king, cringes before worldly powers, shrinks back from trouble and trial, caves in before pressure and opposition and danger. But the eyes of faith look upon this world with different eyes. First, they see a God who is invisible. Others may not see God. Our employers may not see God and may not consider the realities of God's justice and reign in making decisions. Friends and neighbors and family members may not understand the choices Christians make, simply because they are blind to the reality and glory of God. But faith sees God and delivers us from the fear of every other power. It should be our prayer for everyone we know that God would open their eyes, even as we pray that we would see and know and act upon the presence of God in our lives. Seeing him drives out fear, for one mightier than Pharaoh is with us. As the writer of Hebrews will say: "Because God has said, 'Never will I leave you; never will I forsake you.' So we say with confidence, 'The Lord is my helper; I will not be afraid. What can man do to me?' " (Heb. 13:5–6).

Faith allows us to look upon this world and see it as this passage shows us. Ours is a world under judgment; as the destroyer of the firstborn once visited Egypt, so must God's holy wrath visit all the ungodly in the end. That is what the Red Sea waters symbolized, God's judgment pouring over his enemies, destroying them and casting them forever into a dark pit of death. The same waters that saved Israel destroyed the Egyptians, just as the gospel is a two-edged sword (Heb. 4:12; Rev. 1:16). To one it is a fragrance of life but to another the fragrance of death (2 Cor. 2:16). That is what Peter said in his first epistle, referring to Christ as the cornerstone of God's spiritual temple: "Now to you who believe," he wrote, quoting the prophet Isaiah, "this stone is precious. But to those who do not believe . . . 'A stone that causes men to stumble and a rock that makes them fall' " (1 Peter 2:7–8). Here we see the difference between faith and unbelief in the gospel.

The Red Sea waters provide an especially fit symbol of Christ's second coming, as did the waters of Noah's flood. The one event of Christ's return, like the passing of God's people through the sea, will bring blessing on his people at the same time that it brings judgment on their enemies. This is what Paul wrote about to another persecuted group of Christians. Speaking of God's vindication in that day to come, he said:

> *This will happen when the Lord Jesus is revealed from heaven in blazing fire with his powerful angels. He will*

punish those who do not know God and do not obey the gospel of our Lord Jesus. They will be punished with everlasting destruction and shut out from the presence of the Lord and from the majesty of his power on the day he comes to be glorified in his holy people and to be marveled at among all those who have believed. This includes you, because you believed our testimony to you. (2 Thess. 1:7–10)

What a difference faith makes! Now it means the difference between fear and courageous perseverance, the very thing those early Christians needed and we so greatly need today. But it will mean even more on that great day to come when the heavens part as the Red Sea once did and Jesus comes back to bring salvation to his own, to those who trusted in him, and judgment on the world that turned away. "Yes, I am coming soon," he says at the end of the Bible. And all those who look to him in faith, afflicted in this world but not destroyed, cry out in reply, "Amen. Come, Lord Jesus" (Rev. 22:20). Amen.

TWELVE

FAITH
CONQUERING

HEBREWS 11:30-40

These were all commended for their faith, yet none
of them received what had been promised. God had planned
something better for us so that only together with us
would they be made perfect. (Heb. 11:39–40)

In this chapter we come to the last of our Old Testament
studies of examples of faith. These verses that finish Hebrews 11 look back on the last verse of the previous chapter,
where the writer says of these Christians facing persecution,
"But we are not of those who shrink back and are destroyed,
but of those who believe and are saved" (Heb. 10:39). Salvation is by believing; a failure to believe or a shrinking back
from faith because of hardship or opposition leads to judgment and destruction. That is what motivated the writer of
Hebrews in all these studies of faith: not just interesting and
encouraging tales, but a matter of eternal life or death. Now

he briefly offers two last examples, Joshua and Rahab, followed by a list of others whose faith conquered and endured to the end.

THE WALLS FALL DOWN

Verse 30 points to a famous example of faith conquering through God's power, the fall of Jericho under the godly leadership of Joshua. The writer of Hebrews moves forward forty years from his last example, pointedly skipping those who perished in the desert for their rebellion against God, whom he earlier employed as an example of unbelief. Forty years passed after the crossing of the Red Sea, but finally God brought Israel to the promised land. Moses died at the age of 120, and Joshua son of Nun took over as Israel's leader. The Book of Joshua, which tells this account, begins with the transfer of authority. In a famous passage, God gave Joshua his charge to leadership and also to faith: "Be strong and courageous, because you will lead these people to inherit the land I swore to their forefathers to give them. . . . Be strong and courageous. Do not be terrified; do not be discouraged, for the LORD your God will be with you wherever you go" (Josh. 1:6, 9).

Joshua's first challenge was to capture the fortress city of Jericho, which dominated the entrance into the land of Canaan, and for this verse 30 remembers his faith. Joshua's first action toward this objective was to send spies to reconnoiter the enemy position, and these spies would be the vehicles by which Rahab's name is joined to his.

Before the battle, Joshua encountered a mysterious figure who named himself as "the commander of the army of the Lord." Many, I think rightly, identify him as the preincarnate

Christ. First, he stated that the Lord had delivered Jericho into Joshua's hands. But then came instructions that must have seemed bizarre, to have the people march around the city for seven days, on the seventh day blowing trumpets, after which the walls would fall (Josh. 6:3–5). Joshua and the people under him did as they were told, and, just as God had said, when the trumpets sounded, the walls fell down and the Israelites put the city to the sword (Josh. 6:20).

Verse 30 memorializes this event as a great moment in the record of faith: "By faith the walls of Jericho fell, after the people had marched around them for seven days." This is faith trusting the promise of God and obeying carefully the commands he has given. Here we have perhaps the classic portrait of faith drawing forth the power of God, and from it Christians have long drawn the conclusion John Chrysostom expressed in the ancient church: "Assuredly the sound of trumpets is unable to cast down stones, though one blow for ten thousand years, but faith can do all things."[1]

Coupled with Joshua's exploit is the faith of Rahab, the Canaanite prostitute, in verse 31: "By faith the prostitute Rahab, because she welcomed the spies, was not killed with those who were disobedient." Before the battle, Jericho's leaders had detected Joshua's spies, and Rahab hid them at the risk of her life. One commentator says of her: "At the moment . . . there seemed not one chance in a million that the children of Israel could capture Jericho. These nomads from the desert had no artillery and no siege-engines. Yet Rahab believed—and staked her whole future on the belief that God would make the impossible possible."[2] Rahab explained why: "I know that the LORD has given this land to you. . . . We have heard how the LORD dried up the water of the Red Sea for you when you came out of Egypt . . . for the LORD your

God is God in heaven above and on the earth below" (Josh. 2:9–11). Based on that faith, Rahab asked the spies to guarantee her family's survival when the city was taken. She arranged to let a scarlet cord out her window to mark her house, a sign that Christian commentators have long understood as a type of the atoning blood of Jesus. One of the church's earliest commentators, Clement of Rome, wrote that this sign foreshadowed "that through the blood of the Lord all who trust and hope in God shall have redemption" (1 Clem. 12:7).

Joshua and Rahab make quite a pair! In so many significant ways they were wholly different. Joshua was a man, an Israelite, Moses' successor as Israel's leader, the conqueror of Jericho. Rahab was a woman, a member of the cursed Amorite race, a prostitute, and a citizen of the condemned city. They had only one thing in common: they believed on the Lord and trusted his power to save. Centuries later we look back, and none of their differences matter; what counts is their faith and the salvation they thereby entered.

FAITH CONQUERING

At this point, it seems the writer of Hebrews looks where he is in his narrative, scans back over the vast biblical territory he has covered in this chapter, looks forward to all that he hopes to relate, and decides it is time for a change of strategy. It is comforting for me to know that I am not the only preacher whose ambitions are curbed by time constraints and perhaps by the attention span of the audience! Verse 32 tells us, "And what more shall I say? I do not have time to tell about Gideon, Barak, Samson, Jephthah, David, Samuel, and the prophets." Lacking time for these great tales of faith, he merely mentions their names and, in the remaining verses of this chapter, recounts some of the varied exploits of faith. He makes the point that the Old Testament is literally filled with accounts of faith, each of which is enough to inspire us to imitation. This final section may be divided into two categories. In verses 32–35a, we see faith conquering in success over obstacles, and in verses 35b–38, faith is shown conquering through perseverance in great suffering.

Let's begin by perusing this list of six great names. Gideon gave Israel victory over the Midianites with his force of just three hundred men. Obeying God's command he armed them with torches in earthen jars; when the trumpets were blown, they smashed the jars and God threw the enemy into a panic (Judg. 7). Joined to his name is that of Barak, another great leader from early in Judges. Spurred on by the prophetess Deborah, Barak led the united tribes in their victory against Sisera and the mighty Canaanite chariot army.

Next come Samson and Jephthah, also from the Book of Judges. Jephthah's foolish vow cost his daughter's life, but he too was a man of faith. Despite his beginning as an unwanted child and his later career as a bandit, through faith he led the tribes in battle against the Ammonites. Samson was hardly a paragon of virtue; he is particularly known for his fatal weakness for foreign women. Nonetheless he belongs in this list of heroes of faith because of his one-man war against the Philistines, and especially for the way he ended his life, achieving in his death by faith what he had failed to do in his life because of unbelief.

Finally we have two great heroes of the Old Testament, David the king and Samuel the prophet. Samuel's long career as judge and prophet was a crucial one, bridging the years of turmoil under the judges to the early monarchy that he did so much to create. Even his birth tells a story of great faith, his barren mother Hannah crying out to God for help and offering her child to the Lord's service. Without Samuel's faithful ministry, Israel would surely have fallen into total disarray, the Philistines would have subjugated them, and David would have died an unknown shepherd.

The most recognizable name on this list belongs to David, Israel's greatest king, the man after God's own heart (1 Sam. 13:14). David slew the giant Goliath by faith, and his career is one of the main Old Testament types for Jesus Christ. David, though a very great sinner, was also the quintessential Old Testament man of faith.

Having run through this list of names, the writer of Hebrews next turns to the kinds of things faith enabled these and others to do. He organizes the list into three groups of three, starting in verse 33: "Who through faith conquered kingdoms, administered justice, and gained what was promised." The number of warriors on the list of names we considered perhaps leads the writer to first state that by faith they "conquered kingdoms." This could be said of Joshua, David, and Solomon; indeed, victory in battle was probably the most common achievement produced by faith during this early period of Israel's history.

It is possible, however, to succeed in battle without faith in the Lord. Therefore, we read that these heroes "administered justice" as well. The Greek literally says they "established righteousness." This was a hallmark of Israel's faithful judges and kings. They did not merely win battles, but they served God by establishing his righteousness within their domains. This is always a mark of godly leadership, as 2 Samuel 8:15 said of David: "David reigned over all Israel, doing what was just and right for all his people."

Because of faith, these believers "gained what was promised." This phrase is hard to translate precisely, for it could just as easily read that they "received promises" instead of "what was promised." At first glance, it seems best to take the first of these two options. This chapter has continually stressed the point made in verse 39: "These were all commended for their faith, yet none of them received what had been promised." Verse 13 also states that Christian faith looks for promises that will not ultimately be fulfilled until heaven. But at the same time, these heroes of faith did see many promises come true. Joshua saw the walls fall down; Rahab was saved from death; David was made king as promised, and so forth. Remembering this makes it most likely that the verse is speaking about the things these believers did receive through their faith. Their experience encourages us that our faith in the great promises of the gospel will be fulfilled in God's timing just as was theirs.

The second trio of achievements runs from verse 33 to verse 34: "Who shut the mouths of lions, quenched the fury of the flames, and escaped the edge of the sword." David and Samson slew lions, but this seems to refer to Daniel, who refused the king's edict to stop worshiping the Lord. When he was thrown into the lions' den for punishment, God stopped the mouths of the lions and he emerged safe. His three friends Shadrach, Meshach, and Abednego similarly refused to obey a king's command to deny God. When they were thrown in the raging fire, God went with them. He protected them, and they emerged safe. Surely the writer of Hebrews would not mind our remembering their great testimony of faith: "If we are thrown into the blazing furnace, the God we serve is able to save us from it, and he will rescue us from your hand, O king. But even if he does not, we want you to know, O king, that we will not serve your gods or worship the image of gold you have set up" (Dan. 3:17–18).

Verse 34 adds that there were others "whose weakness was turned to strength" through faith. Here Samson comes to mind, having forfeited his strength through folly but regained it at the end through faith. This is a common biblical theme, but one of my favorite examples is that of Jehoshaphat who "became powerful in battle and routed foreign armies." When confronted by a vast enemy invader, Jehoshaphat stood before God in the assembly of the nation. Praising God for his might, he pointed out the threat of the invading armies and concluded, "O our God, will you not judge them? For we have no power to face this vast army that is attacking us. We do not know what to do, but our eyes are upon you." The Scripture continues, "All the men of Judah, with their wives and children and little ones, stood there before the LORD." Jehoshaphat looked to God in his weakness and found strength. The Lord sent a prophet to reply to this great and godly king: "Do not be afraid or discouraged because of this vast army. For the battle is not yours, but God's" (2 Chron. 20:12–15). If that is how God dealt of old, that is how we will find him if only we will look to him in the same kind of faith.

In verses 34 and 35, the writer of Hebrews completes his litany of achievement: "Women received back their dead, raised to life again." This statement speaks of two specific events, one from the ministry of Elijah and the other from Elisha. Elijah had sought shelter with the widow of Zarephath, a woman from pagan Sidon. She had trusted God by obeying the prophet's various commands, and through faith she received this miraculous display of God's blessing (1 Kings 17). In contrast to her, Elisha received help from a wealthy woman who had been unable to bear a child. God blessed her with a son, but when he subsequently died, she sought out the prophet to ask for God's intervention. Through her faith in Elisha's ministry, a ministry so symbolic of Christ's, her son was restored to life (2 Kings 4).

You see the point, that by faith God's people achieve what they never could have done otherwise. In openly miraculous ways and in the more subtle and secret ways, the Lord provides his great power for those who trust in him. We might put this in the form of questions: How are we to overcome great obstacles? How do we who are so weak find the strength our circumstances require? What are we to do to overcome tragedies? The answer to all of these is the same. God's people are to have faith in him, finding deliverance and power and resurrection in the God we believe and trust.

FAITH ENDURING SUFFERING

If the author of Hebrew's account of faith were to stop there, it might leave us with the dangerously false impression that faith keeps us from suffering in this world. You hear this kind of thing today, that if you have enough faith, you need never be sick or poor or troubled in any way. Verse 35, however, refutes such thinking, telling us about "others," that is, people who trusted God and yet were subjected to the greatest of trials. Theirs, however, was no less a conquering faith, for it enabled them to honor God by faithfully enduring to the end:

> Others were tortured and refused to be released, so that they might gain a better resurrection. Some faced jeers and flogging, while still others were chained and put in prison. They were stoned; they were sawed in two; they were put

to death by the sword. They went about in sheepskins and goatskins, destitute, persecuted and mistreated—the world was not worthy of them. They wandered in deserts and mountains, and in caves and holes in the ground. (Heb. 11:35–38)

The first statement is a dramatic one, that some of the faithful were tortured to death and refused to gain their deliverance by denying the faith. The writer probably has the Maccabean martyrs in mind. These were the second-century B.C. Jews who stood up to the Seleucid king Antiochus Epiphanes, who persecuted them by requiring them to eat swine flesh and sacrifice to Greek gods. The apocryphal book of 2 Maccabees provides a description that matches the particular Greek word for torture in our passage, one that means being stretched over a frame and beaten. The scene it depicts was well known in the author's time, the torture and murder of seven brothers in succession, each of whom refused to deny the Lord. The brutal tortures are graphically described and include scalping, mutilation, tearing out the tongue, and frying over the flames, most of which took place while they were stretched over the wheel of a catapult.

As our passage describes, these seven brothers accepted their deaths rather than renounce their faith, specifically because of their hope in a resurrection—a better one than experienced at the hands of Elijah and Elisha, which only restored the dead to this world, but a resurrection to eternal life in the world to come. One of the brothers spat out to his tormentors, "The King of the universe will raise us up to an everlasting renewal of life, because we have died for his laws." The last of the brothers to die confidently turned to the wicked king and assured him that his brothers, though dead, "after enduring their brief pain, now drink of ever-flowing life, by virtue of God's covenant" (see 2 Macc. 7:9, 36 JB).

That kind of sacrifice, that brand of fidelity, is incomprehensible to the person who knows not God. But the eyes of faith reckon it a fair bargain, however unpleasant, even a privilege and honor to suffer for God's sake. Another contemporary Jewish writing puts it like this: "The souls of the righteous are in the hand of God, and no torment will ever touch them. In the eyes of the foolish they seem to have died, and their departure was thought to be an affliction, and their going from us to be their destruction; but they are at peace. For though in the sight of men they were punished, their hope is full of immortality" (Wis. Sol. 3:1–4 RSV).

In verse 36, our passage tells of those who were jeered and flogged, chained and put into prison. We might think of any number of prophets of whom this was true, as it was for our Lord Jesus. Verse 37 speaks of those who were stoned, as were many of the faithful and especially the prophets, or sawed in half—tradition holds that the prophet Isaiah died this way at the hands of wicked king Manasseh—or put to death by the sword, as was the apostle James. "They went about in sheepskins and goatskins, destitute, persecuted and mistreated. . . . They wandered in deserts and mountains, and in caves and holes in the ground." This may have the Maccabees in mind, for this is specifically said about them (1 Macc. 2:28; 2 Macc. 5:27; 10:6), although these things were also true of Elijah and Elisha.

Finally we have this wonderful understatement that says so much: "The world was not worthy of them" (v. 38). The world thought these men and women unfit because of their faith in God, when in reality because of its unbelief this world was not a fit place for them. "Therefore," Hebrews 11:16 tells

us, "God is not ashamed to be called their God, for he has prepared a city for them." How well they remind us, as the apostle John writes, "The world and its desires pass away, but the
man who does the will of God lives forever" (1 John 2:17).

A PANORAMA OF FAITH

If you go to the visitors center at the Gettysburg battle-
field, you will find a panorama depicting what took place there,
a circular portrait within which you may stand to view the
drama as if you were there. That is what our writer has done
for us in these verses. Here, we stand amid biblical history,
among these heroes of faith, and we see what faith brings and
what faith can do. What John said at the end of his first epistle would be a more than fitting inscription: "This is the victory that has overcome the world, even our faith" (1 John 5:4).

We can observe four facets of faith from this panorama.
The first is that what matters is not the circumstances in
which we find ourselves but our faith in God. It ought to be
obvious that Christian faith does not guarantee us comfort in
this world. Yes, God delivers some from trouble, but others
God delivers in trouble. Faithful Elijah was spared Ahab's
wrath, but numerous other faithful prophets died by his
sword (1 Kings 19:10). Jeremiah escaped King Jehoiakim's
hatred, but his fellow prophet Uriah did not escape. If God
sent an angel to break Peter's chains, he also allowed James,
another one of Christ's three closest disciples, to die at
Herod's command. Understand, then, that God may place
you on either of the two sides of this record: on the side of
those who conquered in success or that of those who conquered in defeat. What matters is not the circumstances, neither the blessing in this life nor the trials. What matters is

the faith by which we may conquer in all circumstances through the blood of Jesus Christ.

Second, faith suffices while we wait for God's promises to be fulfilled. It is true that many blessings come to the Christian in this life, yet the great point of this chapter is the one found in verse 39: "These were all commended for their faith, yet none of them received what had been promised." One of the reasons for this is that God's promises are beyond what can be received in this mortal existence. It is not in the flesh but in glory that we will be fit to receive what God has for us. Paul writes, "No eye has seen, no ear has heard, no mind has conceived what God has prepared for those who love him" (1 Cor. 2:9). Thus we are encouraged in our faith, knowing that just ahead lies an eternal weight of glory, beyond the cross there awaits a crown. What do we have while we wait, often in great difficulty? Faith suffices for the man or woman of God, for faith perceives and makes real these things that are yet unseen.

Third—and I think this is the main point the writer of Hebrews had for his original readers—times of trial especially demand faith. We remember that this letter was written to those tempted to fall back because of persecution. Earlier the author reminded them of a time when their heroes suffered some of the things recorded in this passage. Only those who stand firm in faith, even in hardship, are joined to this honor roll of salvation. Indeed, that is what trials do: they test and try our faith, they burn away the dross so that what is left is pure and glorious to God. Jonathan Edwards rightly comments: "The divine excellency of real Christianity is never exhibited with such advantage as when under the greatest trials; then it is that true faith appears much more precious than gold."[3]

In trials, we are encouraged by the knowledge of Christ's suffering for us and of the unbreakable bond created with him through our faith. Thus Paul could write,

> Who shall separate us from the love of Christ? Shall trouble or hardship or persecution or famine or nakedness or danger or sword? As it is written: "For your sake we face death all day long; we are considered as sheep to be slaughtered." No, in all these things we are more than conquerors through him who loved us. (Rom. 8:35–37)

Fourth, and finally, let us remember that in the end, when all else is gone, what will matter is our faith. It is only through faith that we are saved. Look back over this list of names and those associated with these descriptions, and think of the great variety that exists among them. Some were Jews; others were not. Some were rich, and others were poor. Some were men, some were women; some were loved, some were hated; some were successful, some were not. What, then, is it that puts their names on this blessed list of God's beloved? It is only one thing: faith. Realize, too, that someday your life will be looked back upon in the same way we now look back on these lives of others. How insignificant will be so much that we think important now—our clothes, our cars, our houses, our reputations. With faith we gain Christ and his cross, the forgiveness of sin and life everlasting; without faith we are left to perish with the useless things of this world.

Are you rich, are you poor; are you popular, are you despised; are you looked up to or looked down upon? What will it matter, compared with the matter of your faith? Labor, then, for eternal treasure through faith, which above all else is precious, because through faith your souls will be saved.

The twentieth-century martyr Jim Elliot was right when he said: "He is no fool who gives what he cannot keep to gain what he cannot lose."

That is the note on which our passage concludes: "These were all commended for their faith." Literally it says, "These were attested, they had their names recorded, for their faith." In other words, their names are written here only because of their faith, and the same is true in the Book of Life in heaven, where their names are also found. It is only through faith in Christ that we are saved and thus have our names recorded in the list of the redeemed. In the day of judgment that is all that will matter, and faith then will indeed be more precious than gold.

These men and women of faith died without receiving all that had been promised. Verse 40 concludes, "God had planned something better for us so that only together with us would they be made perfect." The key word is "better." It is a key to the Book of Hebrews, which speaks of better things in Christ—a better plan, a better priest, a better covenant, a better sacrifice, better blood, a better home forever. These heroes of faith were waiting to see these better things; what they hoped to see, we have seen through faith in Jesus Christ. You see the point: if they could believe not seeing Christ, knowing only shadows and not the reality, not seeing with anything like our clarity the purchase price of our redemption by the cross, how much more faith ought we to have than they, we who are called by his name? John Calvin writes "A tiny spark of light led them to heaven, but now that the Sun of righteousness shines on us what excuse shall we offer if we still cling to the earth?"[4] Far from concluding from this great chapter that our circumstances make a smaller demand for faith, this argues that our greater privilege brings greater responsibility. In light of the cross of Christ, surely this is how every believing heart must respond, as Isaac Watts puts it:

> When I survey the wondrous cross
>   on which the Prince of glory died,
> my richest gain I count but loss,
>   and pour contempt on all my pride.
>
> Forbid it, Lord, that I should boast,
>   save in the death of Christ my God;
> all the vain things that charm me most,
>   I sacrifice them to [through] his blood. . . .
>
> Were the whole realm of nature mine,
>   that were a present far too small;
> love so amazing, so divine,
>   demands my soul, my life, my all.

THIRTEEN

FAITH FIXED ON JESUS

HEBREWS 12:1–3

*Therefore, since we are surrounded by such a great cloud
of witnesses, let us throw off everything that hinders and the sin
that so easily entangles, and let us run with perseverance the race
marked out for us. Let us fix our eyes on Jesus, the author and
perfecter of our faith, who for the joy set before him endured
the cross, scorning its shame, and sat down at the right hand
of the throne of God. Consider him who endured such
opposition from sinful men, so that you will not
grow weary and lose heart. (Heb. 12:1–3)*

It has been rightly said that the story of our lives is finished
only in the lives of other people, others we have loved and
led, influenced and inspired. The same can be said of the great
eleventh chapter of the Book of Hebrews, that it is finished
only in the chapter that follows, in which the example of
these heroes of the faith reaches out to us. The goal of He-

brews 11 was not mere history but exhortation; that is why Hebrews 12 begins with the key word *therefore*, demanding that we deal with the implications of what we have learned, applying the lessons of their faith to our lives.

THE CONTEXT OF THE CHRISTIAN LIFE

There are four things we should notice from this passage, beginning with the context of the Christian life. It is often said that context is the key to interpretation, so the question is this: What is the context, what is the arena in which you as a Christian should interpret your life? Do you think of yourself living in the midst of a secular society, with its testimony of materialism and sensuality and relativism? Or do you think of yourself as part of a particular corporation or organization, with its mandates to conformity? Do you think of yourself as part of the family in which you grew up, the neighborhood in which you live, a racial group, or a socioeconomic class? However you answer, how you conceive of the context or arena of your life will dramatically shape your manner of living.

The writer of Hebrews suggests something far different from these, namely, that Christians should think of themselves as "surrounded by a great cloud of witnesses" who bear testimony to faith in the Lord. If you are a believer, he says, this is the context in which you should see yourself. This is the body to which you belong and whose approval you should court. This is the audience, as it were, before whom you live, a great arena filled with the beloved of God, the faithful of all ages, and now is the day when you are running your race to the sounds of their approval and encouragement.

This cloud of witnesses, of course, refers to the heroes of

the faith presented in Hebrews 11: Noah, Abraham, Moses, and the others. Sometimes this is called the Westminster Abbey of biblical faith, comparing this chapter with the great church in England where so many of that nation's heroes are buried. But there is a great difference here, namely, that the writer of Hebrews does not see these as dead people to be remembered but living witnesses to be heard. Although they are dead, they are living still, and what was said of Abel can be said of them all: "By faith he still speaks, even though he is dead" (Heb. 11:4). John Owen writes, "All the Old Testament saints, as it were, stand looking at us in our striving, encouraging us in our duty, ready to testify to our success with their applause. They are positioned around us for this purpose, and so we are surrounded by them."[1]

This, then, is how you should conceive of your life. You belong to this noble company of God's people, living in this world but glorifying God through faith. This is the context of your life. You are surrounded by those with whom you will spend eternity, those who will be your brothers and sisters long after everyone else is consigned to judgment. You should hear their voices and conform to the pattern of their faith and not to the pattern of this world.

THE CALLING OF THE CHRISTIAN LIFE

This leads to the second point, the calling of the Christian life. Hebrews 12:1 concludes by telling us that God has marked out a race for us. He has laid out a course for our lives. There are places we are to go, things we are to do, challenges we are to confront. We do not know where this course winds on its way to heaven, nor, frankly, is it important for us to know. Our calling is to "run with perseverance the race marked out for us." Many Christians spend far too much effort trying to figure out what lies ahead, when our calling is to persevere in faith wherever God should lead us.

This metaphor of life as a race was common in ancient literature as well as in the Bible. Paul employs it in 1 Corinthians 9:24–25, where he tells Christians to "run in such a way as to get the prize . . . a crown that will last forever." He describes his life in similar terms, writing at the end of his life to his disciple Timothy: "I have fought the good fight, I have finished the race, I have kept the faith. Now there is in store for me the crown of righteousness" (2 Tim. 4:7–8).

The writer of Hebrews now applies this terminology to us. First, he tells us that the stands are packed with the saints of old. He places them there not merely as spectators but as a cheering section. He tells us to pay attention to their testimony, to heed the encouragement they give us. There is Abel reminding us of the true sacrifice we are to trust. Out cries Noah, that while the world is condemned there is an ark of salvation. Abraham cheers for all who hope for promises yet unfulfilled, just the way he did for so many years in Canaan. Moses cries out to those who, like him, must forfeit status and favor in the world, riches and rank, in order to follow the Lord. Their presence gives us the home field advantage for our race, if we will only see them there and hear their cries.

We saw earlier that the context in which we envision ourselves has a great influence over our thinking, but how we conceive of our calling in life is even more vital. What is the purpose or goal of your life? Is it to attain a certain standard of wealth? Is it to rise to a position of influence and power? Is it to be popular or to enjoy maximum leisure and fun? These are the ways our unbelieving society defines success but not how a Christian should think of his or her life.

Indeed, how liberating it is for a Christian to realize that his or her true calling is the race of faith in the living God: to persevere in the various settings where God will place you, to hold fast your convictions and your obedience to God in different settings and seasons of life, to grow in grace and to glorify God through faith all the way to the end. This is our victory: not worldly standards of success but enduring in faith to the end.

This is not an easy calling, and just as an athlete trains hard, the writer of Hebrews gives us training instructions: "Let us throw off everything that hinders and the sin that so easily entangles."

He speaks here of two things, starting with hindrances. In the ancient Greek games, a runner trained to make his body lean. Then, before the race began, he stripped off his long garments to run naked. The Greek word here for hindrances may be used of excess body weight and of weighty garments. The writer of Hebrews tells us that anything like this, anything that slows us down, must be discarded if we are to run well.

This exhortation helps us with all sorts of decisions about our lives. People will say, "This is not technically a sin, so it must be all right for me." But here we read that anything that weighs you down, anything that hinders your spiritual progress, should be discarded. Perhaps it involves your lifestyle. For instance, many Christians today have bought into the entertainment culture, giving vast hours to mindless television, to unwholesome literature and movies. If this describes you, you should ask yourself, "Is this a help or a hindrance to me spiritually?" Hindrances can be career ambitions, hobbies, associations and friendships, habits and preoccupations. Any of these may or may not be a problem, and it will vary from person to person. But each of us should look at the things in our lives and ask, "Is it a help? Is it a hindrance?" If it is the latter, then the wise believer will let the hindrance go, not wanting to be weighed down in the race.

When we turn to the matter of sin, the situation is far more grave. Hindrances weigh us down, but sin entangles our feet, possibly bringing us down to the ground. Notice how the writer puts it: "the sin that so easily entangles." We take sin lightly at our great peril. Sin is deceitful, as we read in Hebrews 3, able to lead us off the path. Therefore, we must be wise regarding sin, seeking grace from God to be free from sins that we know about, while shunning the temptations to sin that abound.

Think, for instance, how quickly and thoroughly a great man like King David fell into sin when he allowed his heart to lust after Bathsheba. How entangled he became and what a horrible impact that sin had on his life and on his whole family, even the kingdom! He was running brilliantly, as almost no one had run before, but sin entangled him and took him down. Sexual sin and pride continue to entangle the feet of many, including leaders in the church.

Therefore let us flee temptation and oppose all sin. Sin is the agent of death in our world; it is the master of untold slaves. Sin is never profitable, and the pleasures it offers the unwise are all filled with deadly poison. Even true believers, whose debts are paid by the blood of the Lamb, can scarcely afford sin, for we have a race to run, a course marked out by God for these few short years of our lives, and unless we actively shun sin, we will quickly find ourselves distracted and entangled.

This is our calling, the challenging race of a life of faith. Notice what kind of race we run. It is not a short sprint, and we will not finish it with a reckless burst of energy. It is a long-distance race, and our great virtue is not speed but perseverance. Many of us have experienced the flush of excitement at our conversion, only to find that enthusiasm must be converted into endurance. What Jesus said to the church at Thyatira should be true for us as well: "I know your deeds, your love and faith, your service and perseverance, and that you are now doing more than you did at first" (Rev. 2:19).

THE ENCOURAGEMENT OF
THE CHRISTIAN LIFE

This leads to our third point and to Hebrews 12:2, which gives the encouragement of the Christian life. I often call this the all-purpose Christian verse because there is no circumstance, no difficulty, no temptation for which this is not a reliable guide. It says: "Let us fix our eyes on Jesus." This is the secret of the Christian life, the encouragement we need for our faith, to place our eyes not on the world with its enticements and threats, not even on ourselves with our petty successes and many failures, but on him who is the source and fountain of all our spiritual vigor. Owen writes:

> A constant view of the glory of Christ will revive our souls and cause our spiritual lives to flourish and thrive. . . . The more we behold the glory of Christ by faith now, the more spiritual and the more heavenly will be the state of our souls. The reason why the spiritual life in our souls decays and withers is because we fill our minds full of other things. . . . But when the mind is filled with thoughts of Christ and his glory, these things will be expelled. . . . This is how our spiritual life is revived. [2]

The writer of Hebrews has shown us the *context* of our life of faith and the *calling* of our life of faith. Now he sets before us the *encouragement* our faith requires: "Let us fix our eyes on Jesus." As we consider verse 2, we find three ways that this encourages us. First, Christ is the premier example for our faith.

The Greek word translated as "author" is better rendered as "forerunner" or "pioneer." It describes one who goes ahead to blaze the trail and overcome barriers. Similarly, the word "perfecter" connotes the idea that Jesus is the supreme and perfect example of faith, especially since the Greek text speaks of *the* faith rather than *our* faith.

It is noteworthy that this verse focuses on the ordeal of the cross, where Jesus' faith in God was put to the greatest test and given the most brilliant display. The religious authorities said of him on the cross, "He trusts in God" (Matt. 27:43). They were mocking him, yet how true it was. By faith, Jesus pleased God as Enoch did; like Abraham, Jesus looked forward to the city to come and, by faith, was willing to make the supreme sacrifice. By faith, Jesus, like Moses, set aside earthly glory that he might be numbered among the afflicted people of God and become their deliverer; by faith Jesus made the sacrifice Abel's faith presented. If the heroes of the Old Testament are lights testifying to faith in God, Jesus on the cross is a blazing sun bringing faith to its highest expression.

Jesus endured suffering and shame on the cross. The Hebrew Christians were in danger of shrinking back from these very things, just as we find them so difficult to endure. It was by faith that Jesus "endured the cross, scorning its shame," persevering to his appointed end and thus entering into his glory in heaven. He "sat down at the right hand of the throne of God," because he faithfully endured suffering and did not fear the world's contempt. This provides an example for us, that we would bear the cross in our own lives. First Peter 2:21 says, "To this you were called, because Christ suffered for you, leaving you an example, that you should follow in his steps." How important, then, for us to fix our eyes upon him. James Montgomery Boice wrote:

> The only thing that will ever get us moving along this path of self-denial and discipleship is fixing our eyes on Jesus and what he has done for us, coming to love him as a result, and thus wanting also to be with him both now and always. Jesus is our only possible model for self-denial. He is the very image of cross-bearing. And it is for love of him and a desire to be like him that we take up our cross and willingly follow him.[3]

Jesus is our example in perseverance but also in spiritual joy. Our passage says that "for the joy set before him [he] endured the cross." That is an amazing statement, and it says much about his faith. We may conceive of Jesus' joy before the cross in a number of ways. First, Jesus took joy in doing his Father's will. He once said, "My food is to do the will of him who sent me and to finish his work" (John 4:34). William Newell writes, "There is no joy like the accomplishment of a noble task: and of the noblest task of all eternity, Christ was to say, 'I have finished it.' "[4]

Surely, as well, Jesus looked upon his future reunion with the Father in heaven with the greatest of joy. He rejoiced at the knowledge of what his suffering and death would accomplish, namely, the redemption of a people for himself. In short, Jesus rejoiced because he saw the crown beyond the cross, he saw the purchase of his blood, even the church to be his bride forever in the regenerated glory of the age to come. In the same vein, the apostle James writes to us, "Consider it pure joy, my brothers, whenever you face trials of many kinds, because you know that the testing of your faith develops perseverance" (James 1:2–3). We should rejoice at trials, because by enduring we gain the crown that waits beyond the cross.

Jesus is not only the example for our faith but also the object of our faith. He waits at the finish line for us; it is to him and for him that we run. We endure and persevere because we want to know him and join him and share the blessings of his salvation. This again explains why the cross is emphasized here, for the cross is not only the greatest example of Jesus' faith but also the focus of our faith in him. We see his blood shed for our forgiveness, we see the wrath of God spent on him, and we find our safety there, our righteousness at his cross. To be a Christian, then, means to rely on his atoning blood, on his finished work for our salvation, to hold this gospel as the great treasure of our heart. Henceforth we want to be faithful to him, we would please and serve him, and we would endure to the end so that we will spend eternity with him. Therefore Paul says of his ambition: "I press on to take hold of that for which Christ Jesus took hold of me. . . . One thing I do: Forgetting what is behind and straining toward what is ahead, I press on toward the goal to win the prize for which God has called me heavenward in Christ Jesus" (Phil. 3:12–14).

Thus we fix our eyes on Jesus because he is the example and object of our faith. Third, we fix our eyes on Jesus, because he is the source of our faith. It is in this sense that the translation "author and perfecter of our faith" has real merit.

Jesus is not merely an example the way some long-dead hero might be. Nor is he the object of our faith as some mere philosophical ideal. He is an active recipient of our faith, active in inspiring and empowering faith in us because he lives now. Faith in Christ produces union with a living Lord who reigns in the heavens, who is seated at the right hand of God's throne in power. Therefore, when we fix our eyes on him, he works in us by his power, sending God's Holy Spirit to sustain us in our trials. Thomas Watson says,

> As the Spirit is at work in the heart, so is Christ at work in heaven. Christ is ever praying that the saint's grace may hold out. . . . That prayer which Christ made for Peter, was the copy of the prayer he now makes for believers. "I have prayed for thee, that thy faith fail not" (Lk. 22:32). How can the children of such prayers perish?[5]

You see why this exhortation—"Let us fix our eyes on Jesus"—is so important in such a difficult race as ours. Those who fix their gaze on the world and the things of the world will be conformed to its pattern. But in a still more powerful and reliable way, those whose gaze is fixed on Jesus will find themselves changed into his pattern—not merely because of the working of our own hearts but because of his active and transforming work in collaboration with the Holy Spirit. With our eyes fixed on him, we are, Paul says, "being transformed into his likeness with ever-increasing glory, which comes from the Lord, who is the Spirit" (2 Cor. 3:18).

How essential it is that we grasp this principle! As Christians we live in the context of this great cloud of witnesses, with a race to run with endurance, a race that includes the suffering and shame of the cross. You see why, therefore, we must remove every hindrance and entangling sin, for this is already more than the flesh can endure. Yet we are encouraged and empowered in our faith as we look away to Jesus Christ, our great example of faith, the object of our faith, and the source of our faith, its author and finisher, as he reigns with power from on high in us and for us.

If you have never looked to Jesus in faith, if you have yet to enter this godly calling of those who follow him, this exhortation applies especially to you. Look to Jesus Christ, and you will find one who is altogether lovely, whose example of life and death transcends any other, and most important, who suffered death that you might be forgiven and have eternal life. Unless you look to Jesus in faith, you will never know the life that is of God, and although you may enjoy this world for a season, there will be no crown for you at the end but only the judgment of God and the punishment your sins deserve.

A CURE FOR WEARY HEARTS

Fourth, and finally, we find in this passage a cure for weary hearts. This is what Hebrews 12:3 says: "Consider him who endured such opposition from sinful men, so that you will not grow weary and lose heart." Here the writer anticipates a problem and prescribes its cure.

This verse assumes something believers know all too well, namely, that from time to time Christians grow weary and become downcast. If you feel this way, you are not exceptional; this is something you should expect. Especially when faced with prolonged difficulty or trials, even the strongest Christian can experience spiritual depression. The cure for this, he says, is to consider Jesus in his struggle with the opposition of the world.

That may sound the same as verse 2's exhortation to fix our eyes on Jesus, but there is a difference in emphasis here. There, the Greek word *aphorao* meant to look away from one thing to another; the emphasis was to keep looking away from distractions and to fix our eyes on Jesus. Here, in verse 3, the writer uses a different word, *analogizomai*, which means to consider intently. This is an accounting term related to our word *logistics*; when we speak of *logging* something in, we mean that a record should be kept of what transpired. The point is that we should meditate or reflect upon, take stock of Jesus' life and death as it relates to our struggle, and especially remember how God ordained his suffering for his and our glory. We are to remember that beyond the cross there lies a crown; it was so for our Lord, and it will be for us. As Paul writes, doing the very thing our text suggests, "I consider that our present sufferings are not worth comparing with the glory that will be revealed in us" (Rom. 8:18). That is the cure for our hearts when we grow weary in the long race of this life of faith.

How do we consider Jesus? By consulting what the Bible says about him. We read the Gospel accounts and learn what Jesus said and did and how God delivered him. We read the Epistles, which explain the significance of his life and death and resurrection. Indeed, in the Old Testament we see Christ in his work, as he is prophesied and represented by various types and symbols.

This is the very thing we find our Lord doing for his disciples in the Gospel accounts. I think a worthy way to conclude these studies of faith in Hebrews 11, especially as we are reminded here that they all direct us to Jesus, is with an account that appears in Luke 24. There we learn of two downcast disciples walking away from Jerusalem on the day

Jesus was resurrected. They were weary and had lost heart, but unknown to them, Jesus, risen from the grave, came alongside them on the road. Jesus asked what they were talking about, and Luke says, "They stood still, their faces downcast" (Luke 24:17). That is how he finds us sometimes, discouraged and standing still instead of running the race. The two told Jesus about a man from Nazareth they thought would be the Messiah. But, they added, he had been arrested and killed, and they did not understand the confusing reports they had heard about him being seen afterward.

Jesus responded by turning them to the Scriptures. Luke tells us, "Beginning with Moses and all the Prophets, he explained to them what was said in all the Scriptures concerning himself" (Luke 24:27). What Jesus did for them, we are to do for ourselves, seeking and finding him and contemplating his life and ministry in the pages of Scripture.

When the party arrived at their destination, Jesus revealed himself to the disciples and then miraculously disappeared. Yet, in spite of this direct encounter with the risen Lord and his dramatic disappearance, the two now encouraged disciples marveled not at this supernatural experience but at the things they had seen in the Scriptures! "They asked each other, 'Were not our hearts burning within us while he talked with us on the road and opened the Scriptures to us?' " (Luke 24:32).

That is what we will find when our hearts have grown cold on the long and sometimes difficult race that is our calling as Christ's disciples. We open the Scriptures and Jesus teaches us of himself, no less than he did for those two disciples, and as we consider him in his sufferings for us, his victory over sin and death, our hearts too are warmed and even burn within us. That is what makes us rejoice as we should, singing words of confident faith like those from the hymn:

My hope is in the Lord who gave himself for me,
And paid the price of all my sin at Calvary.
For me he died, for me he lives,
And everlasting life and light he freely gives.[6]

If you want to live that way, with that kind of joy and power, then you must fix your eyes on Jesus, not on this world or anything in it, and consider how great a Savior he is. That is the fitting conclusion to this great chapter, Hebrews 11, that our faith must rest on Jesus Christ, our champion and our hope, like the heroes of faith before us, and in whom we find strength for every trial to run with endurance the race God has set before us. To him be the glory.

NOTES

Chapter 1: What Is Faith?

1 John Owen, *Hebrews* (Wheaton, Ill.: Crossway, 1998), 217.
2 Philip E. Hughes, *A Commentary on the Epistle to the Hebrews* (Grand Rapids, Mich.: Eerdmans, 1977), 439.
3 Ceslas Spicq, *L'Epître aux Hebreux*, 2 vols. (Paris: Gabalda, 1952–53); cf. Hughes, *Hebrews*, 439.
4 John Calvin, *Hebrews and 1 & 2 Peter* (Grand Rapids, Mich.: Eerdmans, 1963), 157–58.
5 Watchman Nee, *The Normal Christian Life* (Wheaton, Ill.: Tyndale, 1977), 78–79.
6 Ravi Zacharias, *Can Man Live Without God?* (Dallas: Word, 1998), 192.
7 Cf. J. P. Moreland and Kai Nielsen, *Does God Exist?* (Nashville: Thomas Nelson, 1990), 197.
8 J. C. Ryle, *Holiness: Its Nature, Hindrances, Difficulties, and Roots* (Durham, England: Evangelical Press, 1979), 144.
9 Ibid.

Chapter 2: Faith Justifying

1 John Calvin, *Hebrews and 1 & 2 Peter* (Grand Rapids, Mich.: Eerdmans, 1963), 160.
2 George Whitefield, sermon 14, "The Lord Our Righteousness," in *59 Sermons*.
3 James Montgomery Boice, *Genesis: An Expositional Commentary*, 3 vols. (Grand Rapids, Mich.: Zondervan, 1982), 1:201.
4 Ibid., 1:202.
5 G. Campbell Morgan, *The Crises of the Christ* (Old Tappen, N.J.: Revell, 1903), 392.

Chapter 3: Faith Pleasing God

1 Andrew Murray, *The Holiest of All* (Grand Rapids, Mich.: Revell, 1993), 445–56.

2 A. W. Pink, *An Exposition of Hebrews* (Grand Rapids, Mich.: Baker, 1954), 667–68.

3 Ibid., 668.

4 Thomas Watson, *A Body of Divinity* (Carlisle, Pa.: Banner of Truth, 1958), 53–54.

5 C. Austin Miles, "In the Garden," quoted in Peter Lewis, *God's Hall of Fame* (Ross-shire, U.K.: Christian Focus, 1999), 32.

6 F. F. Bruce, *The Epistle to the Hebrews* (Grand Rapids, Mich.: Eerdmans, 1990), 287.

7 Murray, *The Holiest of All*, 450.

Chapter 4: Faith Working

1 J. D. Douglas et al., *New Bible Dictionary*, 2d ed. (Downers Grove, Ill.: InterVarsity Press, 1982), 382.

2 Cf. James Montgomery Boice, *Genesis: An Expositional Commentary*, 3 vols. (Grand Rapids, Mich.: Zondervan, 1982), 1:258–259.

3 John Calvin, *Hebrews and 1 & 2 Peter* (Grand Rapids, Mich.: Eerdmans, 1963), 165.

4 F. F. Bruce, *The Epistle to the Hebrews* (Grand Rapids, Mich.: Eerdmans, 1990), 286.

5 B. F. Westcott, *The Epistle to the Hebrews* (London: Macmillan, 1903), 358.

6 Philip E. Hughes, *A Commentary on the Epistle to the Hebrews* (Grand Rapids, Mich.: Eerdmans, 1977), 463.

7 Alexander Maclaren, *Expositions of Holy Scripture*, 11 vols. (Grand Rapids, Mich.: Eerdmans, 1959), 10:116.

8 Ray Stedman, *Hebrews* (Downers Grove, Ill.: InterVarsity Press, 1992), 122.

9 Calvin, *Hebrews and 1 & 2 Peter*, 166.

10 Maclaren, *Expositions of Holy Scripture*, 10:119.

11 Peter Lewis, *God's Hall of Fame* (Ross-shire, U.K.: Christian Focus, 1999), 52.

Chapter 5: Faith Looking Forward

1 James Montgomery Boice, *Ordinary Men Called by God* (Grand Rapids, Mich.: Victor, 1982), 18.
2 Arthur Pink, *An Exposition of Hebrews* (Grand Rapids, Mich.: Baker, 1968), 692.
3 Ibid., 695.
4 Philip E. Hughes, *The Epistle to the Hebrews* (Grand Rapids, Mich.: Eerdmans, 1977), 468.
5 Jeremiah Burroughs, *The Rare Jewel of Christian Contentment* (Carlisle, Pa.: Banner of Truth, 1964), 95.
6 John A. MacArthur Jr., *Colossians and Philemon* (Chicago: Moody, 1992), 20.

Chapter 6: Faith in the Promise

1 Donald Grey Barnhouse, *Expositions of Bible Doctrine Taking the Epistle to the Romans as a Point of Departure*, 10 vols. (Grand Rapids, Mich.: Eerdmans, 1954), 4:311–12.
2 J. C. Ryle, *Holiness: Its Nature, Hindrances, Difficulties, and Roots* (Durham, England: Evangelical Press, 1979), 263.
3 Charles Haddon Spurgeon, *A Treasury of David*, 3 vols. (Peabody, Mass.: Hendrickson, n.d.), 1:172, 178.
4 A. W. Pink, *An Exposition of Hebrews* (Grand Rapids, Mich.: Baker, 1954), 650.
5 Jeremiah Burroughs, *The Rare Jewel of Christian Contentment* (Carlisle, Pa.: Banner of Truth, 1964), 82–83.

Chapter 7: Faith Seeking a Home

1 John Murray, *The Epistle to the Romans* (Grand Rapids, Mich.: Eerdmans, 1968), 139.
2 Thomas Watson, *A Body of Divinity* (Carlisle, Pa.: Banner of Truth, 1958), 296–97.
3 Charles Haddon Spurgeon, *Spurgeon's Sermons*, 10 vols. (Grand Rapids, Mich.: Baker, n.d.), 1:229.
4 Charles Haddon Spurgeon, *Metropolitan Tabernacle Pulpit*, 63 vols. (Carlisle, Pa.: Banner of Truth, 1971), 31:139.
5 Cyril C. Richardson, ed., *Early Christian Fathers* (New York: Collier, 1970), 217.

6 Venn, announcing the death of his wife; cf. J. C. Ryle, *Holiness: Its Nature, Hindrances, Difficulties, and Roots* (Durham, England: Evangelical Press, 1979), 190.

7 John Bunyan, *Pilgrim's Progress* (Nashville: Thomas Nelson, 1999), 13.

Chapter 8: Faith Tested

1 John Owen, *Communion with God* (Carlisle, Pa.: Banner of Truth, 1994), 17–18.

2 A. W. Pink, *An Exposition of Hebrews* (Grand Rapids, Mich.: Baker, 1954), 745.

3 William L. Lane, *Hebrews 9–13* (Dallas: Word, 1991), 360.

4 Pink, *Exposition of Hebrews*, 748.

5 Philip E. Hughes, *The Epistle to the Hebrews* (Grand Rapids, Mich.: Eerdmans, 1977), 482.

6 Cf. Hughes, *Hebrews*, 485.

7 Peter Lewis, *God's Hall of Fame* (Ross-shire, U.K.: Christian Focus, 1999), 86.

Chapter 9: Faith Trusting God's Plan

1 William L. Lane, *Hebrews 9–13* (Dallas: Word, 1991), 365.

2 John Calvin, *Hebrews and 1 & 2 Peter* (Grand Rapids, Mich.: Eerdmans, 1963), 175.

3 John Powis Smith; cf. Martyn Lloyd-Jones, *The Life of Joy* (Grand Rapids, Mich.: Baker, 1989), 103–4.

4 Philip E. Hughes, *The Epistle to the Hebrews* (Grand Rapids, Mich.: Eerdmans, 1977), 487.

5 Peter Lewis, *God's Hall of Fame* (Ross-shire, U.K.: Christian Focus, 1999), 94.

Chapter 10: Faith Choosing God

1 Charles Haddon Spurgeon, *Metropolitan Tabernacle Pulpit*, 63 vols. (Carlisle, Pa.: Banner of Truth, 1973), 34:534.

2 G. A. F. Knight, *Theology as Narrative* (Edinburgh: Handsel Press, 1973), 57–58; cf. Peter Lewis, *God's Hall of Fame* (Ross-shire, U.K.: Christian Focus, 1999), 102.

3 J. C. Ryle, *Holiness: Its Nature, Hindrances, Difficulties, and Roots* (Durham, England: Evangelical Press, 1979), 138.

4 Charles Haddon Spurgeon, *Metropolitan Tabernacle Pulpit*, 63 vols. (Carlisle, Pa.: Banner of Truth, 1973), 34:466.

5 Ryle, *Holiness*, 139.

6 Spurgeon, *Metropolitan Tabernacle Pulpit*, 34:465.

7 William Barclay, *The Letter to the Hebrews* (Louisville, Ky.: Westminster/John Knox, 1976), 157.

Chapter 11: Faith Passing Through

1 Peter Lewis, *God's Hall of Fame* (Ross-shire, U.K.: Christian Focus, 1999), 105.

2 Philip E. Hughes, *A Commentary on the Epistle to the Hebrews* (Grand Rapids, Mich.: Eerdmans, 1977), 150.

3 Ibid., 151.

4 John Owen, *Hebrews* (Wheaton, Ill.: Crossway, 1998), 233.

Chapter 12: Faith Conquering

1 Cf. Philip E. Hughes, *A Commentary on the Epistle to the Hebrews* (Grand Rapids, Mich.: Eerdmans, 1977), 502.

2 William Barclay, *The Letter to the Hebrews* (Louisville, Ky.: Westminster/John Knox, 1976), 161–62.

3 Jonathan Edwards, *The Religious Affections* (Carlisle, Pa.: Banner of Truth, 1986), 21–22.

4 John Calvin, *Hebrews and 1 & 2 Peter* (Grand Rapids, Mich.: Eerdmans, 1963), 185–86.

Chapter 13: Faith Fixed on Jesus

1 John Owen, *Hebrews* (Wheaton, Ill.: Crossway, 1998), 242.

2 John Owen, *The Glory of Christ* (Carlisle, Pa.: Banner of Truth, 1994), 167.

3 James Montgomery Boice and Philip G. Ryken, *The Heart of the Cross* (Wheaton, Ill.: Crossway, 1999), 182.

4 William R. Newell, *Hebrews* (London: Oliphants, 1947), 403.

5 Thomas Watson, *A Body of Divinity* (Carlisle, Pa.: Banner of Truth, 1958), 281.

6 Norman J. Clayton, © 1945, 1973 by Norman Clayton Publishing Company. All rights reserved.

DISCUSSION QUESTIONS

Chapter 1: What Is Faith?

1. Read Hebrews 10:36–39. Identify warnings, commands, and promises. How do these verses shape our expectation of what we will read in Hebrews 11?

2. What are the four meanings of *hypostasis*, which Hebrews 11:1 uses to describe faith? Does any of them recall your own experience?

3. The author speaks about what faith does and what faith is. How does he explain these? What experience have you had with these things?

4. What experience did God use to bring you to faith, and what has he done subsequently to grow your faith?

5. How do we distinguish biblical faith from the notion of faith as "a leap in the dark"?

6. The opening paragraph says, "Faith is the issue on which . . . salvation depends." Do you agree or disagree with that statement? Explain.

7. Pray for each other that God may increase your faith.

Chapter 2: Faith Justifying

1. Explain the difference between the sacrifices brought by Cain and Abel. Why was one accepted and the other rejected?

2. What is the difference between justification by faith and justification by works? Why does God accept the one and not the other?

3. Read Genesis 4:6–7 and Romans 1:18–25. According to these passages, why do people have no excuse for not obeying God?

4. How did the symbolism of the tabernacle, the mercy seat, and the cherubim point forward to the work of Christ? What do they tell us about the way of salvation?

5. Cain thought that he could "silence" faith by killing Abel. Why was this assumption mistaken?

6. The chapter argues that it is God who prescribes the right way to worship him. What are the implications of this for our worship today? How are we to decide the manner in which we worship God?

7. What difference does it make to be justified by faith?

Chapter 3: Faith Pleasing God

1. How is the order of the accounts of Abel, Enoch, and Noah suggestive of an order to the Christian life?

2. Practically speaking, what does it mean to walk with God? Can you think of other Bible passages that help you to understand this?

3. According to Hebrews 11:6, what are the two elements of true faith?

4. Verse 6 says, "Without faith is it impossible to please God." Why is this? What are ways in which we try to please God without faith? Why doesn't that work?

5. What are some present and future benefits we gain through faith in this life?

6. Perhaps, unlike Enoch, you feel that God is distant or even absent from your day-to-day life. What steps can you take to

seek God and to walk with him? If you seek God through faith in Jesus Christ, why can you be confident that he will find you?

7. Pray, asking God to help you know him better and to walk with him by faith.

Chapter 4: Faith Working

1. Read Genesis 6:5–18. Why was the flood sent? How did Noah differ from his contemporaries?

2. In what way did God demand more of Noah's faith than he does of ours today? What assistance does our faith have that Noah's lacked?

3. Explain how Noah's faith could produce both salvation and condemnation. How was it both an appeal to sinners and a cause for their judgment?

4. Use Noah's ark to describe the relationship of faith to works. Why are they inseparable?

5. Consider your own beliefs. In what ways do your works demonstrate your convictions: at work? in friendships? in your family?

6. The author states, "Biblical obedience does not fetter you." Yet Jesus describes the Christian life as a narrow path. How can this be? How is obedience to Christ liberating? Discuss this and support your position by Scripture. Compare Psalm 1.

7. What portions of God's Word have recently produced the most growth in your life?

8. How is righteousness the inheritance of those who trust in Christ?

Chapter 5: Faith Looking Forward

1. Why is Abraham called "the father of all who believe"?

2. Was Abraham called because he was a good man? If not, how do we explain his calling? If Abraham was not called because of his works, then on what basis did God call him? How is Abraham's call a picture of the way God calls us to salvation?

3. God called Abraham to leave many things behind. What will/has it cost you to follow Jesus and be a Christian? Are there things you are finding hard to leave behind?

4. The author compares Abraham to what Peter says at the beginning of his first epistle. How do the words *pilgrim* and *chosen* define the Christian life?

5. Imagine Abraham looking out from his tents at the settled cities of Canaan. How is this similar to the way the Christian lives in the world today? What promises sustained Abraham? What promises in the Bible sustain you in your pilgrimage?

6. What difficulties have you experienced in your "Pilgrim's Progress"? How has the vision of "the city with foundations" sustained you along the way?

7. Read Revelation 21:22–22:5. How does this picture of our destination in Christ encourage you in the difficulties of your life?

8. In light of your discussion, pray for one another, asking God to inspire you with the vision of his city with foundations.

Chapter 6: Faith in the Promise

1. This chapter describes Abraham's great sorrow. What was it? What made this sorrow so hard for him?

2. The author speaks of the one thing we lack embittering us in spite of so many blessings. Have you experienced this? Why do we feel this way? What is the answer to this challenge?

3. According to the author, what are two reasons why God deals with his people through promises? Do you have any experience with this?

4. Abraham and Sarah found it hard to wait for God's promise to come true. What did they do to take matters into their own hands? What are ways in which we act similarly? What is the result? How should we wait upon the Lord?

5. The author describes ways in which churches "bear illegitimate children," as Abraham did through Hagar. Is there a difference between being "successful" and being faithful as a church? If we are faithful to God's way of worship, evangelism, and growth, will the church lose out?

6. Romans 4:20–21 provides a classic statement of what faith is all about. How does it relate faith to confidence in God's power?

7. How is God's promise to give a child through the barren womb of aged Sarah a sign of salvation by grace alone? How does our salvation similarly confound human expectations and leave all the glory to God alone? How does Sarah's barren womb point to the virgin birth of Christ?

8. Pray that God would give you faith in light of things that you lack. Ask him for grace to wait upon the Lord.

Chapter 7: Faith Seeking a Home

1. Have you had a mentor in the Christian faith? How has he or she been a help to you? What Bible figures particularly inspire your faith or set a helpful example for you?

2. The heroes of the Bible mostly died without receiving the things they hoped for? Why is theirs not a tragic story? Why is ours not a tragic story if we trust in God all the way to the end of this life?

3. Do you find it unpleasant to think about your own death? How does our faith in Christ transform fear of death into hope of glory?

4. This chapter describes Christians as aliens in this world. Is it possible to follow Christ without this happening? Does being an alien mean that Christians can't relate to other people?

5. How important is it for Christians to know what the Bible says about life after death? Can you cite passages that speak to this matter?

6. Reflect on the statement, "God is not ashamed to be called their God." How can the Bible say that of people who have shamed themselves with sin? Discuss the significance of this statement in terms of your attitude toward the trials of this life.

7. Pray for yourselves and for others who are facing the reality of death. Pray for God's grace to live as aliens in this present world.

Chapter 8: Faith Tested

1. What is the most difficult test your Christian faith has endured? What did you learn from the test?

2. The author says that God's command tested Abraham's relationship with him in terms of his devotion, his spiritual understanding and his knowledge of God. Consider what God demanded from Abraham and discuss these aspects of his obedience.

3. Many people are repulsed by the thought that God would make such a demand as the one we read of here. Does God have a right to do this? Does it speak poorly of his character? If not, why not?

4. The author imagines that Abraham must have spent a long night in prayer before obeying this command. What is the role of prayer in response to the testing of our faith?

5. Should we obey God's commands even if we don't understand them? Why or why not? How do we gain understanding in difficult matters of obedience?

6. How is the episode atop Mount Moriah a "parable" of the atoning death of Jesus Christ? Can you recite the striking parallels between Abraham's offering of Isaac and God's offering of his Son? More importantly, how does the cross shed light on God's motives toward us?

7. How is your faith being tested now? How does the message of this passage help you to say along with Abraham and Jesus, "Your will, not mine, be done"? Pray for God to strengthen you in the difficult matters of obedience.

Chapter 9: Faith Trusting God's Plan

1. Why do you think God gave Abraham insight into what was going to happen in years to come after his death?

2. What was wrong with the way Jacob went about seizing the things God had promised him? Do you struggle with grasping things the way he did? What is a better alternative? Discuss.

3. Jacob's life was not always lived by faith in the Lord. But according to this chapter, he ended his life well. How does his request to be buried in the Promised Land, a request he made "as he leaned on the top of his staff," speak of what was best in Jacob's faith?

4. Here we have three generations of faith, all of them trusting God's promise and plan. In what ways do we pass on the faith from generation to generation today? Do you have any contact with the generation before or after you? What kind of impact does this make on your life?

5. The author says, "God's plan centers on the work of Jesus Christ for the salvation of sinners." What do you understand about that plan? Can you support your understanding from Scripture?

6. How does God's plan relate to you? What role do you have in the advancement of God's plan?

7. Peter Lewis points out that God's plan cannot be manipulated, cannot be taken for granted, and cannot fail. Do you ever act as if these things were not true? How do these comments correct our foolish thinking?

8. The author remarks on the crossed arms of Jacob as he blessed Joseph's sons and speaks of God's "cross-purposes" in the world. What does he mean? What does that say about our expectations of God?

Chapter 10: Faith Choosing God

1. How is your faith revealed through your choices? Does faith really require both a yes and a no? Give examples of each as you have experienced them.

2. How is Moses' choice an accurate advertisement for Christianity? Why would anyone want to do what Moses did?

3. Is it true that Christians often give a false portrait of the Christian life in their evangelism? What should we tell people about Jesus Christ and the life of faith in him? If we tell the truth, how can we expect them to be converted?

4. Do you think Moses was a fool to give up all that he did? What calculations did he make that informed his choice? What kind of calculations do you make and what is the arithmetic of faith in your life?

5. What are the arguments that might have deterred Moses from the choice of faith? Do you have similar voices telling you not to put God first? How does Moses' example help you to respond?

6. Why does the phrase "with the people of God" transform every trial and affliction? How is "with the people of God" linked to "for the sake of Christ"? How does this inform the way you should live?

7. Pray for each other and people you know who are faced with difficult choices that test their faith.

Chapter 11: Faith Passing Through

1. The author describes the exodus as the dominant Old Testament paradigm for Christian salvation. How does Israel's progression in the exodus illustrate the Christian life?

2. Moses was able to overcome his fear of worldly powers because he saw "him who is invisible." How do we "see" God and how does this give us courage and strength?

3. Moses spent forty years living in power and privilege and then forty years waiting in obscurity. Discuss what you know about these two periods of Moses' life and how God used each to shape his future ministry. How does this relate to what God is doing or has done in your life?

4. Describe what happened in the first Passover. How does this point forward to the saving work of Jesus Christ?

5. What does the passage of Israel through the Red Sea tell us about God? Which of his attributes are displayed in that episode? What does it tell us about how we are to trust the Lord?

6. Describe Moses as a leader. What was it that made him effective? What do you see in Moses' leadership that you could apply to your life?

7. The author compares the passage through the Red Sea to the second coming of Christ. Why is this an apt comparison? How does this inform us about the world in which we live and the meaning of our lives?

Chapter 12: Faith Conquering

1. In what ways were Joshua and Rahab different from each other? In what essential way were they similar? What does their fellowship in salvation say about life in the church today?

2. The fall of Jericho is a famous example of the triumph of faith. What was God trying to demonstrate by having the people

march around the walls for seven days? What does this experience tell us about obeying God's Word even when we don't quite understand it?

3. The author of Hebrews mentions Gideon, Barak, Samson, Jephthah, David, and Samuel. Briefly, who were these people and what do their lives show us about faith conquering?

4. Some people today teach that if you really trust the Lord, you need never know suffering or want or difficulty. Assess that teaching in light of this passage? Why is it so dangerous?

5. According to this passage, Christians may equally triumph in success or in failure. How do you feel about the idea of finding victory in apparent defeat? What is it that transforms our thinking about trials and suffering and even persecution?

6. The writer of Hebrews seems to mention the Maccabean martyrs. What do you know about this period of Israel's history? How does their faith in the resurrection set an example for us?

7. The author states that these examples show that our circumstances are really not that important. Is that realistic? What, then, is it that really determines our happiness and success in the Christian life?

Chapter 13: Faith Fixed on Jesus

1. Why does this statement from Hebrews 12 regarding Jesus Christ belong in a study of Hebrews 11?

2. This chapter describes the *context* of the Christian life. What picture is presented here, and how does it relate to your situation?

3. Do you believe that God has marked out a course for your life? Why or why not? How does this affect your attitude and your decision making?

4. What is the difference between a hindrance and a sin? What effect do they have on our lives? What sorts of hindrances do you encounter and how might you "throw them off?"

5. The author refers to Hebrews 11:2 as "the all-purpose Christian verse." How is "fixing our eyes on Jesus" a helpful encouragement in every situation?

6. What does it mean that Jesus is the "author and perfecter" of our faith? How does the author explain these terms, and how do they help us understand what it means to follow Jesus?

7. What joy could Jesus possibly have had "set before him" as he approached the cross? What does the expression mean, "there is a cross before the crown"? How does this inform us about our own discipleship to Jesus?

8. Do you find yourself "growing weary" or "losing heart" as a Christian? What is the antidote to spiritual fatigue, according to this chapter?

9. Pray to God, thanking him for all you have learned in this study of Hebrews 11 and especially for the courage and hope we find through Jesus Christ.

INDEX OF
SCRIPTURE

INDEX OF
SUBJECTS AND
NAMES

Gideon, 176, 177
Gilgamesh epic, 46
glory, 150, 185, 201
God
    command of, 116–17
    eternal plan of, 126, 133–39
    as holy Judge, 40
    promises of, 81–83
    relevance of, 39
    sovereign grace of, 57, 63–64
    wrath of, 57, 164–65, 170
Goliath, 160, 178
grace, 39, 46, 48, 63–64, 88–89

Hagar, 83–84, 85, 86
Hannah, 178
heaven, 35, 43, 69
heavenly city. See city of God
hindrances, 193–94, 200
history, 139
holiness, 12
Holy of Holies, 24–25
Hughes, Philip E., 4, 50, 68, 118,
    137, 164, 165
humanism, 115–16
humiliation, 79
hypostasis, 4–6

idolatry, 39
Ingersoll, Robert G., 107
inheritance, 55, 56–57, 67, 72,
    75, 91, 104, 105, 108
Isaac, 89, 109, 112–13, 118,
    119–20, 127, 132, 135, 138
Isaiah, 183
Ishmael, 83, 85, 127
Israelites, 101–2, 157, 166

Jacob, 127, 128–30, 132,
    135–36, 138
James, 50, 183, 184
Jehoiakim, 184
Jehoshaphat, 180
Jephthah, 176, 177
Jeremiah, 184
Jericho, 174–76
Jesus Christ
    blood of, 19–21, 164, 176
    as center of God's plan,
        133–34
    death and resurrection of, 49
    exaltation of, 139
    as example of faith, 195–98,
        200
    as High Priest, 27
    joy of, 197–98
    as lamb of God, 120–22, 165
    lifted up, 167
    as object of faith, 198, 200
    opposition to, 200
    sacrifice of, 28–29
    second coming of, 170–71
    as source of faith, 198, 200
    suffering of, 155, 186, 196–97
Jochebed, 146
John of Damascus, 167
Joseph, 127, 129–31, 132,
    135–36, 138, 168
Josephus, 146
Joshua, 174–76, 178, 179
journey. See pilgrimage
joy, 97, 197–98
judgment, 40, 46, 58
justification by faith, 3, 11, 19,
    22–23, 29, 62, 93–94

Richard D. Phillips (B.A., University of Michigan; M.B.A., University of Pennsylvania; M.Div., Westminster Theological Seminary) is minister of preaching at historic Tenth Presbyterian Church in Philadelphia. He is also speaker-at-large for the Alliance of Confessing Evangelicals and host of *The Bible Study Hour* radio program. He leads the Reformation Societies, a grass roots endeavor to mobilize Christian leaders across the nation in support of biblical reformation.

An officer in the United States Army for thirteen years, Phillips commanded various tank and armored cavalry units and served as assistant professor of leadership at the United States Military Academy, West Point, before resigning with the rank of major.

He is the author of *Mighty to Save: Discovering God's Grace in the Miracles of Jesus, Encounters with Jesus: When Ordinary People Met the Savior,* and *The Heart of an Executive: Lessons on Leadership from the Life of King David.* He lives in Philadelphia with his wife, Sharon, and their three children, Hannah, Matthew, and Jonathan.